BOB EDWARDS

Fridays with Red

A Radio Friendship

SIMON & SCHUSTER

New York · London · Toronto · Sydney · Tokyo · Singapore

SIMON & SCHUSTER
Rockefeller Center
1230 Avenue of the Americas
New York, New York 10020

Designed by Irving Perkins Associates
Manufactured in the United States of America

1   3   5   7   9   10   8   6   4   2

Library of Congress Cataloging-in-Publication Data

Edwards, Bob, date.
Fridays with Red: a radio friendship/Bob Edwards.
p.   cm.
Includes bibliographical references and index.
1. Barber, Red, 1908–1992.   2. Sportscasters—United States—
Biography.   3. Radio and baseball.   4. Edwards, Bob, date.
I. Title.
GV742.42.B34E38   1993
070.4'49796'092—dc20
[B]   93-27809
                                        CIP
ISBN: 0-671-87013-0

*This book is dedicated to the **real** writer in the family*
SHARON KELLY EDWARDS
and to some future writers
BREAN CAMPBELL
SUSANNAH KELLY EDWARDS
ELEANOR FLANNERY EDWARDS

Acknowledgments

SARAH BARBER GAVE HER BLESSING to this project and told me to write an honest book about her father. She set the example for honesty with her generous recollections. I look forward to sharing stories with her for many years to come.

NPR producer Mark Schramm provided audio tape, anecdotes, memories, encouragement and so much more. It was Mark who made those Friday visits with Red reach their full potential, especially in Red's final year. I am a lucky man to enjoy the benefit of his talents and his friendship. Thanks, Slugger.

In addition to being an ace studio technician at NPR, Arthur Halliday Laurent is a Macintosh wizard who makes house calls. He demonstrated that a patient teacher can deal with the most hopeless case of computer illiteracy. You're a pal, Art.

Besides Red, my other great career mentor is Edward Bliss, Jr. I could fill this page with names you would recognize from among Ed's former students. I am still his student and I thank him for editing an early draft of the manuscript.

Thanks to Charles Rembar, who made the book happen, and to Jeff Neuman, its editor. Jeff is not responsible for any of its flaws.

Many thanks to my family, friends and listeners who

offered support, particularly Ottie Barber, Stanley Beers, Bill Buzenberg, Max Cacas, Sean Collins, Joyce Dewsbury, Gloria Donadello, Gene Ellis, Mary Louise Ellis, Bob Ferrante, Chris Fullerton, Tom Goldman, Barry Gordimer, Andy Hanus, Madison Hodges, Rick Jarrett, Jay Kernis, John Kiesewetter, Steve Kirsch, Ketzel Levine, Ralph Lowenstein, Kee Malesky, John Ogulnik, Rob Robinson, Chuck Thompson, Mark Tucker, Carl Van Ness and Effie Virginia Wynne.

As always, I'm grateful to the staff of *Morning Edition,* which tries its best to make me sound intelligent.

Finally, I want to mention my mom, Loretta Edwards, because she didn't get mentioned anywhere else. Thanks, Mom, for all the times you've told total strangers who have never heard of NPR that I'm your son.

Bob Edwards
Arlington, Virginia
April 1993

Contents

Red Barber with Bob Elson, broadcasting the 1939
World Series for the Mutual Broadcasting System.

Introduction

RED BARBER BELIEVED he had the longest broadcasting
career in American history. He was on the air for almost
sixty-three years. Six decades of talking into a microphone
should reveal everything about the speaker, but in Red's
case they did not. I don't pretend to have "known" Red
Barber, though I spoke with him every week for almost

twelve years. Perhaps no one really knew Red, with the possible exception of his wife, Lylah. Men of Red's generation did not give up their secrets easily, and I respect a man who didn't use the forum he was given to impose on our privacy by sacrificing his own. In this book, I will report on the Red Barber I saw and heard, and loved immensely.

Red was short and thin all his life. By the time I met him in the early 1980s, he was so frail it seemed a gust of wind might take him away. I sensed that if I wasn't careful I might accidentally bump into him and knock him down. This physical frailty contrasted with a mind that worked better and faster than that of almost anyone I have met. Red was less of a redhead by this time, though there was still a hint of orange amidst the gray. His most outstanding feature was his smile. Actually, he had a bunch of smiles. They ranged from the "cat that ate the canary" smile to the broad, unencumbered laugh of the man who just won a poker hand.

In retirement, he and Lylah were well dressed, but not the way they were in their New York years. Their only child, Sarah, recalls that fashion was important to both of them. Red's broadcasting protégé, Vin Scully, says Red was a meticulous dresser, and photographs of Red back up that testimony. In the early 1930s, Red wore white linen suits to auditions at the big stations in the Midwest. The gimmick worked; when WLW in Cincinnati needed a sports announcer, station management could not recall Red's name, but they remembered the young Florida man who wore white linen suits.

Sarah Barber also says her parents were very private people who, in the last two years of Red's life, frequently were uncomfortable having guests visit their home. I believe that was true, although they made me feel welcome when I was there. Their upbringing would not have allowed them to be anything but cordial to guests, but I sensed that I was to behave myself and leave at a respectably early hour. Conversation was warm yet formal; once I spent some time with the Barbers, this didn't seem like a contradiction.

Red was washing dishes when I arrived one evening. Did I show up too early after their dinner? I had not wanted to get there too late and keep them up. He was generous with the bourbon and asked me all about my life and career. He was always interviewing and rarely volunteered information about himself.

Is it possible for a very private man to enjoy being a celebrity? I didn't think so until I met Red. He loved shaking hands and talking with his adoring public. I saw this in his public radio years, and Sarah says it was also true in the days when the New York cabbies would hail him on the streets. Passers-by who saw him wanted to chat, and he didn't brush them off. The recognition went with the job, and whether he enjoyed it or just felt it was his responsibility, he was nice to his fans. A listener wrote to me about the time he recognized Red on a beach. This person made his timid approach to Red, who invited him to join in a stroll along the shore. Others told me of Red's kindness in similar situations.

I've heard many stories of Red's taking time to talk with children about their plans for life, perhaps suggesting they should have such plans. He often gave books as presents to the children of friends and associates. One man told me about a tour his son had been given of the Barber home, with special attention paid to the study where Red did his NPR broadcasts. Red showed the young man how he prepared and took him through the steps of a Friday broadcast. I heard from a woman who, as a little girl, told Red she had never seen a ball game. Red said that had to be corrected, so he showed up at her house and took her to Ebbets Field on a streetcar.

The Barbers had style and flair. In 1975, when Red's brother, Billy, was dying, he told Red he was leaving him twenty-five thousand dollars and instructed Red to "blow it"—maybe on a frivolous trip or something like that. Red used the cash to buy a green Mercedes-Benz. The vanity plate: RED 1. That car achieved notoriety of its own. Some Floridians told me they had never met Red, but they spotted the famous green Mercedes in various parking lots. In the fall of 1991, I asked him how RED 1 was doing. He said he had just had it serviced and the mechanic wanted to buy it from him. But when Red died, the Mercedes died, too; Sarah could not get the thing to move.

Style and flair had their limits. One time we met for lunch in Tallahassee. My expectations were high—out on the town with the Ol' Redhead, a man whose books told of toasts made and deals sealed in places such as Sardi's, Toots Shor's and Louis & Armand's. But this lunch was served in one of those cafeterias featuring tuna salad with cottage cheese on lettuce leaf and carrot shavings locked in Jell-O glob. I think this had less to do with Red's wallet than it did with his stomach, most of which was surgically removed in 1960; on the other hand, it could have had a lot to do with the wardrobe of his public radio guest that day.

During the thirty-three years that he broadcast major league baseball games, it was difficult for Red to have a peaceful meal in a public place. He was asked for autographs, introduced to fellow diners, stared at, pointed to and whispered about. Radio celebrities once ranked with movie stars, and Red Barber was one of radio's biggest stars. Sitting in this Florida cafeteria, he was many years and many miles removed from the watering holes favored by Broadway stars, TV moguls and newspaper columnists. No one stopped by our table to buy us a drink and tell us about some recent success or imminent project.

To look at this little old fellow was to figure that whatever might be special about him was now in his past. But listeners to *Morning Edition* on National Public Radio knew better. They knew that each Friday morning Red Barber talked to them about the important and the trivial, and made both entertaining. For the four minutes that Red was on the air each week, millions of people stopped whatever was making noise, and listened. They listened to hear what the Ol' Redhead was going to tell Colonel Bob regarding the weather in Tallahassee, the garden in his backyard, highlights from the world of sports, tales of those who triumphed over adversity or laments for those who failed tests of character.

Red Barber moved people. A microphone was his magic wand. Either he knew what people cared about or he made them care simply because he had raised the subject. It seemed to me that no one was indifferent to him or what he had to say. He knew how to reach listeners in a way that no one else on radio could. "Unique" is a word often misused. It means "one of a kind." Red was unique.

Red with Jackie Robinson in 1947, when Robinson was the National League Rookie of the Year.

The Beginning

"DADDY, who is Red Barber?"

Late in 1979, Arthur J. Levine, a Long Island CPA, heard this question from his daughter, Ketzel, sports producer for *Morning Edition*, a new program on National Public Radio. He was not surprised. For weeks he had wondered why those geniuses at NPR assigned sports duties to a young woman whose life had been devoted to music. And now she was asking about the man who had been the "verce" of the Brooklyn Dodgers. Levine, a plumber's son, grew up playing punchball in the streets of Crown Heights. When he was a boy, the Dodgers were marvelous entertainers and mediocre ballplayers—but they were Brooklyn's. And the Dodgers got better around the time the games were picked up by the radio and announced by the fellow with the Southern accent.

Morning Edition had begun on November 5, 1979. Ketzel Levine's job was to fill two four-minute sports segments each day. For February, Black History Month, Ketzel wanted a story on the most prominent figure in black sports history, Jackie Robinson. The more research Ketzel did on Robinson, the more Red Barber's name kept popping up. Thus the question:

"Daddy, who is Red Barber?"

Arthur Levine told his daughter that Red Barber was a hero, a man who defied his heritage and treated a black man as a human being. If, in 1947, Brooklyn fans had been asked whether they wanted a black ballplayer, major league baseball's *first* black ballplayer, they probably would have said no. But Robinson achieved that distinction, and this Mississippi-born white man on the radio treated Robinson as if he were the equal of Pee Wee Reese or Dixie Walker. Arthur Levine told his daughter that Red Barber was no rich liberal's kid but was from a working-class family and had inherited all the same prejudices as his peers. Red had confronted that ugliness within himself and triumphed over it. He sent a signal to the fans in Brooklyn and elsewhere in baseball: black ballplayers were to be accepted. Integration was here to stay.

Ketzel Levine had never heard her father speak so enthusiastically about anything or anybody. She called Red Barber, whose first words to her were: "Ketzel—isn't that Yiddish for 'kitten'?" She wondered, how did he know that? Wasn't she always having to explain her name, even to Jewish people? There was little that Red Barber didn't know about cats and a lot of other subjects. She interviewed him as part of a Jackie Robinson story for Black History Month. Ketzel knew good radio when she heard it, and Barber had it all—the knowledge, the charm, the wit, the accent and the storyteller's sense of drama and timing. She invited him to do a commentary each week for *Morning Edition*. Red declined. He said the Social Security laws discouraged employment by placing a cap on the wages one could earn while receiving benefits. The cap was removed when a recipient turned seventy-two.

Months passed. On December 14, 1980, Elston Howard died. Howard had been the first black to play for the New York Yankees. The Yankees were one of the last big league teams to integrate, and for years Howard was their only black player. He would have been a starting player on many teams, but for the Yankees he was a reserve catcher and outfielder. He finally became a regular in 1961 and won the American League Most Valuable Player award in 1963, the first black player to do so. Ketzel wanted to do his radio obituary and thought once again of Red Barber. She knew that Red had left Ebbets Field in Brooklyn for Yankee Stadium in the Bronx after 1953, so he was the Yankee announcer when Howard joined the team. Ketzel interviewed Red on the life and career of Elston Howard, and when it was over Red told her he was now seventy-two and the Social Security salary cap was no longer a problem. He asked if the offer of a regular slot on *Morning Edition* was still on the table. It was.

She invited Red to record a commentary each week at WFSU-FM, the public radio station in Tallahassee, where Red was living. NPR had just become the first broadcasting network to send its signal to the audience by satellite. WFSU just happened to be one of the sixteen stations with an uplink, meaning it could feed to the network a signal of quality equal to that of the signal it was receiving from the network. So Red's tapes would not have to be mailed to

NPR or sent by phone; they could be fed to the network by satellite and would sound great. But Red Barber was having none of this tape business. He wanted to do a live conversation with the program's host. That was *real* radio.

A line was installed to Red's house. Red's voice would travel from the microphone in his study to WFSU and then be uplinked to NPR. We would have an introductory conversation on New Year's Day 1981 to interest listeners in what was to come. Then Red and I would talk for four minutes every Friday at 7:35 A.M., eastern time. There would be more than six hundred Fridays before we were through.

I wasn't always the Colonel. At first Red called me Bob or Robert, which he pronounced "Robbit." Frequently I was "young fella," occasionally "buddy" and sometimes "son." I liked that one. But in 1985, my native state got around to conferring its honorary title on me. When Red heard about it, "the Colonel" was born.

The Honorable Order of Kentucky Colonels is not a terribly exclusive outfit. There must be millions of "Colonels." I've always suspected that even victims of Kentucky speed traps are made Colonels on the spot, though I've never actually witnessed it. All one has to do to be "commissioned" is to have a member of the organization notify the governor's office. Once the governor has sent the commission, the new Colonel not only is entitled to all the benefits of the honor but must share in the responsibilities. I've heard that these responsibilities include returning to Kentucky to defend the Commonwealth from attack, presumably by Ohio or some other Yankee precinct. Privileges include the right to contribute to the organization's charities; the right to buy insignia belt buckles, beer mugs and other swell merchandise from the Colonels' slick catalogue; and the right to have barbecue with the governor during Kentucky Derby week. The barbecue costs each Colonel some money, and is an event of such importance that in 1992 the governor didn't even bother to show up.

Indiana honors a distinguished visitor by making him or her a Sagamore of the Wabash. Maryland commissions one an Admiral of the Chesapeake. Kentucky makes one a Colonel.

I was not the first Colonel in Red's life. In his Dodger broadcasts Red had referred to Brooklyn shortstop Pee Wee Reese as "the little Colonel." Reese was also captain of the Dodgers, so there probably was some confusion about his rank. But Reese, like me, is from Louisville, where he began his professional career with a team called the Louisville Colonels.

Nicknames are important to ballplayers and broadcasters. Duke Snider once told me that his father did him two great favors: he taught him to bat left-handed and he gave him the nickname Duke. Snider made great use of both assets in Brooklyn, where "the Duke of Flatbush" could take aim at a short right-field fence and park many a homer onto Bedford Avenue. It was Red Barber who gave Dolph Camilli the nickname El Capitán and made Dixie Walker "the people's choice." In Brooklyn that became "the people's cherce," just as Carl Erskine became Oisk.

So now I had a nickname assigned to me by no less than Red Barber. This is a good thing to happen to a serious news anchor. It's another little safeguard against ever taking myself too seriously. The only burden is having to explain it to people who think I'm a retired military officer. But in time I think I *became* the Colonel. I became a confident, professional host of the most popular program in public radio. And Red had plenty to do with my maturation as a broadcaster and with the growth of *Morning Edition*'s audience.

Opening Day

MORNING EDITION HAD BEEN A YEAR in the planning before its first broadcast on November 5, 1979. National Public Radio had never before taken such a systematic approach to a project; NPR did extensive research into how people listened to radio in the morning and what type of program would hold their attention. But somewhere along the way, the careful preparation broke down. Days before the inaugural broadcast, a pilot program was produced, and it was awful. NPR veterans and member stations listening on closed circuit agreed that the new program was nothing to which NPR could attach its name. The best way I can describe it is to say that it was very chatty and resembled a bad talk show in a small market. I was thrilled not to be part of such a disaster. I was then a co-host with Susan Stamberg of *All Things Considered*, the afternoon drive-time program that ruled the NPR roost at the time. This new program, if successful, posed a threat to our status and would have required us to share NPR's precious resources. When we heard how bad the *Morning Edition* pilot had been, Susan and I just had a good laugh.

But NPR's member stations had promoted *Morning Edition*. They had promised their listeners that a wonderful new program was coming their way on November 5, so NPR had to provide something by that date, and it had to be quite a bit better than the pilot. NPR management responded by doing something it rarely does: it fired people, in this case the producers and the hosts. Replacements were recruited from other programs.

On October 27, I was preparing a half-hour report for *All Things Considered* on the fiftieth anniversary of the stock market crash. In mid-afternoon, a management delegation came into my office to ask if I would host *Morning Edition* for just thirty days until they could find someone else. Well, I wanted to be a team player. And thirty days didn't sound so long, although it meant getting up each day at 1:30 A.M.

Morning Edition's first program was not a network embarrassment, though it was far from the program you hear today. *Morning Edition* survived the shakedown period of the first year thanks to its dedicated and hardworking staff and the commitment of NPR's member stations, most of which were enjoying their first measurable morning audiences thanks to the new program from NPR. *Morning Edition* was a hit. We were on our way.

The thirty days I agreed to host *Morning Edition* have become fourteen years. I enjoyed working with Susan on *All Things Considered*, but *Morning Edition* allowed me to do something on my own. I had never taken many chances in my career, but here was an opportunity to be part of a program that might someday be worthy of comparison with NPR's older magazine. Besides, I had sort of fathered the baby and I couldn't turn it over to a new dad.

Despite the encouraging words from stations, NPR executives and listeners, I was not content. I was sleep-deprived and I had a lot of anxieties. I have every nervous habit you've ever heard of, and some you haven't. For example, I don't remember ever having fingernails. Broadcast journalism is not a profession for the insecure or the anxious. It's like taking up golf to relieve stress. Now I was being asked to talk live each week with one of the founders of my profession, a living legend. Sure, bring on the Ol' Redhead. But how would I talk to him with my heart in my throat?

On January 1, 1981, I told the *Morning Edition* audience that the American hostages in Iran were in the 425th day of their captivity; Israel and Syria had an aerial dogfight the day before; Henry Kissinger was visiting Somalia and said he would tell incoming president Ronald Reagan all about it; Greece joined the European Community that day; and it was J. D. Salinger's sixty-second birthday. Ninety minutes later I welcomed Red Barber back to broadcasting and asked him if he had missed it.

> RED: I have missed radio . . . far more than television. Winston Churchill once said that he was a child of Parliament. I'm a child of radio. I started at the University of Florida radio station in March of 1930 and I was for years and years in radio long before there was any television. I was very fortunate to do the first big league ball game that was ever done on television. So I was able to grow into the new medium. But radio was always a joy, because the radio broadcaster . . . is the entire show outside of an occasional sound that comes in under or around his voice. The listener only gets what the broadcaster tells him. And you are free at a microphone to just cover the whole playing area, cover the grandstands. You paint the picture . . . the radio announcer is the supreme—the complete artist. And that is satisfying to the human ego. But in television, instead of being the supreme artist, you become the servant of the monitor screen. And the announcer becomes a commentator for that picture in front of him in order that he synchronizes what he says with that picture that the viewer receives. So it's an entirely different kettle of fish. Instead of being the artist, you are then the servant of any number of people and any number of cameras. . . .

BOB: There's a good description of how you call a game in *The Boys of Summer*, Roger Kahn's book. . . . He says, "A ball game told by Barber was a drama, with plots and subplots, but going onward, always onward among stories rounding out scenes, and climaxes described with such dramatic restraint that you cried out, 'Come on, Red, come on, Old Friend, Companion of a Hundred Afternoons, let go, come *root* with us.' " You weren't much of a rooter.

RED: No. I did everything I could not to be a rooter, Bob, because I felt at times at the microphone I was describing to millions of people who could not see the event for themselves what the event was. And I felt it was up to me to describe what happened to the ball and to the people who touched the ball, and then let each listener in his or her way have whatever rooting interest they wanted to have.

That interview, which had been taped over the phone earlier in the week, was broadcast on a Thursday. We ran the rest of the interview the next day in what became Red's regular Friday slot. In this segment I asked Red what he wanted to accomplish in our Friday talks.

RED: Television took away pretty much the individuality, the personality, of the broadcaster, as well as his initiative. . . . And I am glad to have this opportunity to visit with you on a spontaneous basis in which . . . we are turning the clock back and going back to the early days of radio, with its immediacy, with its spontaneity and with its excitement.

It was a good start. And Red's words were prophetic: our conversations were immediate, exciting and spontaneous. I had no problem with the immediate and exciting aspects, but I did not court spontaneity. And after that first taped interview, all but one of the remaining talks with Red were live.

The host of *Morning Edition* works within an extremely demanding format at a ridiculous hour of the day. Timing has to be precise. There's no margin for error. The program is two hours long and the host flies solo; there's no co-host to help carry the load.

In the program's early days, the burden was much worse. NPR had fewer reporters then, and the reporters we had preferred *All Things Considered* because some segments of *Morning Edition* are pre-empted by local stations. With fewer reporters filing fewer stories, the host had to fill the airtime. Our executive producer at the time was Frank Fitzmaurice, a man who loved live interviews. On the morning after Reagan's first election, Fitzmaurice had me do thirty live interviews in a single program. I hated live interviews. A taped interview can be made perfect through editing; a live interview offers no second chances. In a taped interview, the interviewer can focus totally on the content. In a live interview, the interviewer is listening to hear if his question has been fully answered, forming a decision on whether a follow-up is necessary or whether he should move on to another subject, assessing whether the conversation is covering the ground his producers and editors wanted it to cover, watching the clock to see if there's time to cover all that ground, guessing whether the next question will elicit a short or long answer and keeping in mind what comes *after* the interview: a time check, the weather, an introduction to another story—which is it? That's a lot to think about even if the interviewer has had a full night's sleep.

Spontaneity is great if one is an experienced, confident, professional anchorman. By 1981 I would have said that all those adjectives applied to me, but I would have been fooling myself. Our senior producer, Jay Kernis, did the best he could with me. He was good at masking my faults and accentuating my talents. By the time Kernis left NPR for CBS, I had, I hope, improved.

Kernis established a number of procedures for *Morning Edition* staff members to follow—procedures to help me do a better job of hosting the program. Every word I was to say was written down, even my name. Nothing was left to chance. I suspect he told everyone to assume that I didn't have a brain in my head and had not slept for four days. The drill was precisely what I needed, and it made us all better radio journalists because it trained us to take care of details. I didn't want a spontaneous program, I wanted a *safe* program. And here was Red Barber offering spontaneity!

The Colonel and the Redhead in Tallahassee, Florida, October 1990.

Pleasantries

IN BROADCASTING, time is precious. It's no less precious in public broadcasting, even though the absence of commercials gives us more of it. Consequently, a broadcast conversation does not observe the good manners of a normal conversation. On the radio, two people might say, "hello," "good morning" or whatever, but they don't engage in the normal small talk that precedes the business. There's no "What ya been up to?" or "How's the family?" in a radio news interview. If Red Barber knew this, he paid no attention to it. Red was a true Southern gentleman. Good manners were something he got from his mother, and there was no compromising them for radio.

Our Friday conversations were only four minutes long, but Red was determined that they were going to begin with the proper exchange of felicitations. This meant that it was useless to introduce him with a news lead or a question. For example, I might say, "There was plenty of action in last night's Dallas/Washington game. Let's bring in Red Barber and learn what he thought about it. Red, the Cowboys and Redskins are one of the NFL's best rivalries, wouldn't you agree?" But Red's first words would be "Good morning, Bob. It's a bit of a rainy morning down here in Tallahassee. But it's been kind of a dry spring so far, and we could use some rain. Now, about that football game . . ." Eventually, I gave up and did it his way. What else could I do? I began each conversation with "Commentator Red Barber joins us now from Tallahassee, Florida. Red, good morning."

Red usually opened by describing the weather. That was no problem for me. Any fool can handle a weather conversation, and *this* fool always made certain to look out the window just before it was time to talk to Red. But then the conversation turned to the garden, and the garden is a foreign country to me. I know more about nuclear physics than I know about plants and flowers. I enjoy their beauty, but I am mostly ignorant of their names and other distinguishing characteristics. Some I knew: dogwoods, azaleas and daylilies are common to both Tallahassee (Red's home) and Arlington, Virginia (my home). I know what they look like and I think they're lovely. But most of the others elude me. Red learned that a storm had left a tree limb embedded in the roof of my house. He asked me what kind of tree it was. "Green," I replied, exhausting every fact I knew about that tree. Red seemed surprised that someone wouldn't know the identity of a tree in his very own yard. Later I was reprimanded by a listener who wondered why I gave that nice Red Barber such a smart-aleck answer when he asked me a perfectly nice question. With just a bit of gardening knowledge I could have made a real contribution to all those talks with Red. But they might not have played as well.

I wasn't the only garden illiterate. Jim Angle filled in for me one Friday and was determined to hold up his end of the conversation with Red. He studied sports all week. By Friday he was armed with scores, statistics, facts, figures and questions. He would be ready for Red Barber. When the time came, Jim wished him a good morning and heard Red say: "Good morning, Jim, and I have just one word for you—wisteria." That was not the word Jim expected to hear. He never recovered.

Red and I talked about the caladiums and the amaryllis. Thanks to Red, I'll always remember that the watermelons are ripe when the crape myrtles are in bloom.

The plant most often discussed was the camellia. Red had thirty camellias in his yard. When he died, his ashes were buried in a cluster of five camellia plants. In the tribute I gave Red on *Morning Edition*, I said, "One of the great voices of America will speak to us no more, and somehow the camellias will never smell as sweet." At least five people wrote to me saying the camellias will never smell at all because they have no scent. One of them added that Red would have kicked my butt for the inaccuracy. (I should have been more specific: the sasanqua has a strong fragrance, and Red had one in his front yard. He told me that the sasanqua is the ancestor of the camellia.)

Some years ago, Sharon Edwards took me by the hand and marched me out to a green bush in our backyard. Pointing to a flower, Sharon said, "Do you see that? That's a camellia. When Red talks about camellias, tell him you have one, too." I do absolutely everything my wife tells me to do. When I told Red about my camellia, he wanted to know what kind. "Pink," I said. Well, this just wouldn't do. He wanted to know its name. I said, "Fred, or Frank—I don't know, Red, it just bloomed and we haven't really got to know each other yet." He started naming types of camellias. Was it, for example, a Julio Nudzio? I resisted the temptation to ask if Julio Nudzio was not the scrappy young second baseman just up from the Mexican League. Instead, I promised to photograph the blossom and send him a picture. When he got my camellia photo, he took it to a Tallahassee nursery for identification and told the audience all about it the next Friday.

We talked about camellias so often that the American Camellia Society honored us with certificates of appreciation. Eat your heart out, Dan Rather! When Red announced this to our audience I told him I was not worthy of the honor and that Red was the head camellia of the act.

It is a tribute to the eccentric charms of Red's segment on *Morning Edition* that far more people remember the camellias than anything either of us said about sports. It may have been part of the pleasantries, but it was hardly routine. The talk about the weather and the garden helped set the scene; Red was more intimately alive to listeners who could see in their mind's eye what Red was seeing as he spoke to me. Red was observing the courtesies of conversation, but he also was applying the lessons of a lifetime in radio.

William Lanier Barber, Red's father, about 1908, the year Red was born.

The Redhead

WHY DID RED BARBER ACCEPT the invitation of Ketzel Levine to become a commentator on *Morning Edition*? He had been everywhere and done everything. He had nothing to gain, nothing to prove. Judging from the content of his work over the next twelve years, he had no axes to grind, either. At first I thought he came aboard because we asked. And maybe because he had missed radio. In the end, I concluded that he wanted to tell *his* story, *his* way.

Walter Lanier Barber was born on February 17, 1908, in Columbus, Mississippi. His father was a railroad engineer. His mother was a schoolteacher who read Greek and Roman mythology to her children. Her father and grandfather had run the newspaper in Columbus until, as Red put it, "bad judgment and good whiskey" did them in. When the boll weevil killed the cotton crop in Mississippi, the Southern Railway had less work for Red's dad. William Barber landed a job with the Atlantic Coast Line and, near the end of World War I, when Red was ten years old, the family moved to Sanford, Florida.

Selena Martin Barber, Red's mother, about 1908.

The tourist-postcard Florida didn't exist yet. This was the wild, cracker Florida described in the books of Marjorie Kinnan Rawlings. The Barbers' modest, two-story home in Sanford still stands and looks well cared for. Sanford was a truck farming area; Red's high school baseball team was called the Celery-Feds. Red was active in football, baseball and track. A good student, he had the highest average in his class. He also read a lot and eventually wanted to become a college professor, though he had a brief flirtation with life in a minstrel show; Red was hired, but the troupe folded before he could join them.

After graduating from high school, Red worked for two years doing highway contruction and other jobs. Then he worked his way through two years at the University of Florida as a janitor and a waiter. He liked having ROTC drills three days a week because wearing the uniform meant he needed to buy clothes for just four days a week. After working all summer following his freshman year, Red lost all his money when his bank failed just two weeks before the fall semester began in September 1928.

Red was one of the few people to have a pleasant memory from the fall of 1929. Red had a friend who drove a bakery truck. One Saturday, they went on a joyride with some buddies, all fortified with a bit of moonshine. The bakery truck overturned and Red was hurt. His pals took him to the university infirmary. When student nurse Lylah Scarborough opened the door, she saw a young man covered with blood and cake icing. "Take him back and lay him down," she said. On Monday he returned with flowers. A year and a half later, on March 28, 1931, they began a marriage that lasted more than sixty-one years.

By then Red had launched his radio career. He was fascinated with the new invention. The marvel of instantaneous communication over long distances without the use of wires is lost on later generations. In Sanford, Florida, a kid named Merrill Roberts had built his own radio receivers and invited young Red to listen. Red would later write:

A man spoke in Pittsburgh, said it was snowing there, and I heard it instantly in Merrill Roberts' house in Sanford, Florida. Someone touched the keyboard of a piano in Kansas City. Somebody sang in New York. A banjo plunked in Chicago. And Merrill Roberts and I heard it instantly. It was sleeting in Atlanta. Rain in New Orleans. When I walked home in Central Florida, it wasn't even cool.

At first Red didn't see radio in his future. Maybe that had something to do with the programming on WRUF, the campus station at the University of Florida in Gainesville. The station carried a farm program on which agriculture professors read their scholarly papers. One day it fell to a man named Ralph Fulghum to read the papers of three professors who were out of town. He begged Red to go to the station with him and read the middle paper so the same voice wouldn't be heard reading all three. Red had no interest until Fulghum promised to buy him dinner. Red Barber's first radio broadcast consisted of his reading a paper titled "Certain Aspects of Bovine Obstetrics." Years later, Red observed that "as I read it, I got the suspicion that the prof who wrote it never intended to be in town on the day the paper was scheduled to be broadcast." Major Garland Powell, the station manager, told Red how well he'd done and asked if he wanted to work for the station. Red did not. Powell persisted and wanted to know what kind of money it would take for Red to give up his other jobs and join the station staff. Red reached for the most outrageous figure he could imagine. "Fifty dollars a month," he said. "It's a deal," said Major Powell, and a sixty-two-year broadcasting career began on March 4, 1930.

For the next four years Red did the news, interviewed

professors, spun records and even sang along with the
Orange Grove String Band. "It was cracker music and an
old cracker boy up there talking," he said later. He also did
lots of sports. Red traced his hatred of basketball to his
broadcasts of the Florida state high school tournament for
three consecutive years. Every school in the state partici-
pated and every game was broadcast. They began at 8:00
A.M. on a Friday morning and ended late on Sunday night.
By then, he said, he was ill. Red fared better doing the
football games of the University of Florida Gators, though
he was not an immediate success. When the University of
Alabama helped Florida dedicate a new stadium in Gainesville, Red got excited as the Gators drove toward Alabama's
goal. He said there was an upset in the making. At that
moment, the Crimson Tide sent in their first team, the one
Red's Alabama spotter had told him was out there all
along. 'Bama won easily and went on to shut out Washington State in the Rose Bowl. Red learned several things
that day: don't take sides, do your homework and be careful in deciding whom to trust. By the time he left Florida
for Cincinnati in 1934, he was ready for the big towns and
the big leagues.

FM radio wasn't fully developed commercially until the
1970s. Until then, a young radio broadcaster longed to
work for one of the big, clear-channel AM stations whose
signals reached hundreds of miles at night. Red and I
broke into radio thirty-eight years apart, but we both had
the same ambition: we wanted to work for WHAS in Louisville or WLW in Cincinnati. Red auditioned at both stations, plus stations in Atlanta and Charlotte. He took a bus
to Chicago once, but he couldn't get past the receptionist
at WGN. Those were Depression years and jobs were few,
but Red's persistence paid off in 1934, thanks to a chain of
events taking place in Cincinnati and involving two men
whose influence would dominate the course of Red's career: Larry MacPhail and Branch Rickey.

When the Cincinnati Reds' owner, Sidney Weil, went

Red interviewing Cincinnati manager Bob O'Farrell aboard an American Airways plane bound for Chicago, June 9, 1934. It was the first time a baseball team traveled by plane.

broke, control of the team reverted to the bank that held the ballpark's mortgage. Not knowing how to run a baseball team, the bank sought advice from Rickey, who was then running the St. Louis Cardinals. Rickey suggested that the bank hire the man who used to run the Cardinals' farm club in Columbus, Ohio. That's how Larry MacPhail entered major league baseball.

One of MacPhail's first tasks was to convince Powel Crosley to assume majority ownership of the Reds and serve as president. Crosley manufactured automobiles, refrigerators and radios, but MacPhail was after more than the security of Crosley's money. Crosley also owned two radio stations, including WLW, a boomer of a station whose signal reached so much of the country that it boasted of being "the nation's station." MacPhail wanted Crosley's stations

to broadcast the Reds' games. At that time, most teams
didn't broadcast their games; baseball executives reasoned
that people would not go to the ballpark to pay for something they could get for free on the radio. MacPhail knew
better because his team in Columbus had broadcast its
games; broadcasting actually stimulated interest in the
team.

WLW's airtime was considered too valuable to be devoted to baseball games. Besides, its signal was "national."
So the Reds' games were to be carried on WLW's sister
station, WSAI, a five-thousand-watt station with a "local"
signal. Neither station had a play-by-play announcer, but
someone remembered the Florida boy in the white linen
suit. On March 4, 1934, Red's fourth anniversary with
WRUF in Gainesville, he received a telegram from Cincinnati asking if he would broadcast the Reds' games for
twenty-five dollars a week. He accepted and was instructed
to report to "Scotty Ruston" in Tampa, where the Reds
were in spring training. The telegram contained a typo:
"Scotty Ruston" actually was the team's road secretary,
James "Scotty" Reston, whose career as a journalist for *The
New York Times* was still ahead of him.

After several weeks of getting to know the Reds, the
young broadcaster was off to Cincinnati. "And nobody
bothered to ask me, Bob, if I'd ever done a big league ball
game or a professional game. Sometimes it's very wise, like
being a good witness, not to volunteer anything." In fact,
the first game Red broadcast in Cincinnati was the first
major league game he had ever seen. He didn't even know
how to fill out a scorecard. That game on opening day in
1934 almost made news for another reason: Cubs pitcher
Lon Warneke took a no-hitter into the ninth inning, when
Adam Comorosky scratched a single. Red's first game
nearly was a no-hitter.

When former pitcher Waite Hoyt died in August of
1984, Red told my vacation replacement, Scott Simon, how

Hoyt had figured in the Ol' Redhead's early days in Cincinnati.

RED: There is no such thing as a self-made man. We are all the repository of many other people and many other events. When I was a green-pea announcer in Cincinnati in 1934—I had just done three major league ball games when the Pittsburgh Pirates came to town. Waite Hoyt was with them then. And I was sent down to the hotel to get some ballplayers to go on a radio program. And I didn't know one ballplayer from another. So I went into the lobby of the hotel and I would ask people, "Are you with the Pittsburgh Pirates?" And I asked a big, florid-faced man, and he said, "Yes, I'm George Gibson, the manager." And then he lit into me—just a tirade, very profane, very loud, right there in the crowded lobby. Apparently he was mad about something, mad about radio. But he stunned me. I didn't know what to say. Then he stepped on the elevator and left.

And there I was. I figured I'd better give up and go back to Florida. And suddenly, two big men got up from a sofa and came over. One of them said, "I'm Waite Hoyt. I'm a pitcher." He said, "Gibson had no right to talk to you that way. This is Fred Lindstrom. We will go with you and go on your radio program." Well, when somebody picks you up like that, Scott, it is extremely pivotal. Instead of being a crushed young announcer, maybe losing a job, suddenly I had confidence again. That was a marvelous pick-up.

Hoyt and I continued our friendship over the years. And when I went to New York to broadcast the Brooklyn games in 1939, he did a pre-game and a post-game radio show before and after the play-by-play. And after two years, he got the chance to go back to Cincinnati to be the play-by-play announcer. And he came to me and he said, "Red, being a ballplayer, I didn't learn how to score. I've got this job in Cincinnati, but I've got to learn to score. Will you teach me?" So I had the satisfaction of knowing that Waite Hoyt was scoring the way I scored all the years that he was such a distinguished broadcaster.

Another thing about Hoyt I'd like to say is that for years he was a very important drinker. And then he went to Cincinnati, and after he got into severe trouble, he became [a member of] AA. And he became a head man in the AA. And they tell me that you could call at two or three o'clock in the morning and he'd get up and go help some troubled soul. So Hoyt was a great soul, was a great man. And he did the hardest single thing that a human being can do: he defeated himself.

The Reds were not much of a team on the field, but MacPhail was making things happen. He had Red broadcast interviews three hours before the start of the game to spur people's interest in going out to the ballpark. He installed a farm system. MacPhail was the first general manager to put his team in an airplane for road trips. (Red did interviews from the plane while the first flight was in the air.) He cleaned up Crosley Field, installed more rest rooms and tried to attract what were then called "ladies" to the games (the women who could be found at ballparks back then were not to be confused with "ladies"). And it was Larry MacPhail who started night baseball in the major leagues on May 24, 1935. President Franklin D. Roosevelt threw a switch that fired up the lights at Crosley Field in Cincinnati. Red Barber was at the microphone and remembered the "ooohhs" of the crowd.

RED: Yes, I was the resident announcer at Crosley Field in Cincinnati. Larry MacPhail installed the first lights against the objections of pretty much everybody in baseball. He had the support of the commissioner, however, and he got it going. And baseball has never been the same.

BOB: Yes, they used to play a lot of day games.

RED: That's right, and one of the people who was most outstanding in saying that baseball should be played in the daylight, et cetera, and it was against tradition to have it at night, et cetera, was the late Clark Griffith, who had the Washington Senators. As soon as he saw that crowd in Cincinnati that night, he suddenly realized something. And he went back and he became the advocate of unlimited night baseball.

BOB: Well, what were the fears? Obviously that batters couldn't see the ball, or that, I guess, fielders couldn't see the ball either.

RED: That was it, and also baseball has been very conservative, very right-wing on the part of the owners. They said it was against tradition, that you were supposed to play in God's sunlight.

BOB: Of course, they didn't have television then or they would have had night ball a lot sooner. . . .

RED: . . . Nobody was even thinking about television in 1935. But that was the first sporting event that was ever on the Mutual Broadcasting network. That was a network then of four stations: WGN in Chicago, CKLW in Detroit, WOR in New York and, of course, the mighty, half-million-watt transmitter of WLW in Cincinnati.

WLW's affiliation with the Mutual Broadcasting System was to pay big dividends for Red. The new network broadcast the World Series in 1935 and teamed WLW's Red Barber with WGN's Bob Elson. Red was just twenty-seven years old and in only his second season as a big league broadcaster, but he already had the best assignment in sportscasting. The other networks had their stars working that series; Boake Carter was there for CBS and Lowell Thomas for NBC.

After baseball season was over, Red broadcast University of Cincinnati football games and some of Ohio State's games. On his trips to Columbus, he watched Jesse Owens on the track, where Owens was preparing for the 1936 Olympic Games. When Ohio State played Notre Dame that year, both teams were undefeated; the game attracted enormous national attention and WLW had exclusive rights to the broadcast. The networks put pressure on WLW to surrender exclusivity. The station relented, but not until the game was just three days away. Mutual picked up Red's broadcast for WLW. Ted Husing was the CBS broadcaster. NBC sent Bill Slater. The Irish, led by quarterback Bill Shakespeare, capitalized on Buckeye mistakes and rallied in the final minute to win, 18–13.

Red also got to work the 1936 World Series, where he finally met his hero, Graham McNamee, who had done the first World Series broadcast in 1923. Red's partner for the Series was Tom Manning, who broadcast the Indians' games in Cleveland. They rode to the Polo Grounds in McNamee's black Cadillac, not bothering to stop for red lights; Red said McNamee must have known every cop in town. During the game, Red gave the cue for a station break as the two teams switched sides between innings. Then he felt a hand on his elbow turning him to his left. McNamee, who had been watching and hearing Red work, said to him, "Kid, you've got it." Red counted this as his moment of arrival in the business. McNamee and Husing virtually had invented play-by-play radio sports in the 1920s, and now Red Barber, ushering in a second broadcast generation, was their peer, swapping stories with his elders over drinks. Cincinnati would not hold him much longer.

The twenty-three-year-old rookie announcer at WRUF in Gainesville, Florida, in 1930.

Barberisms

A RED BARBER BROADCAST was a piece of Americana, and artists in other fields paid tribute. At various times, Red was the announcer on radio shows featuring the big bands of Sammy Kaye and Woody Herman. Woody's "herd" played a number called "Red Top" in honor of Red Barber.

For the higher of brow, there was a musical composition Red and I discussed on my thirty-ninth birthday, May 16, 1986:

BOB: Forty-five years ago today, WOR in New York first played *A Symphony in D for the Dodgers* by Robert Russell Bennett. And you figure into this history a little later that summer. You narrated it at a performance at the Lewisohn Stadium by the Philharmonic Symphony Orchestra, Wilhelm Steinberg conducting.

RED: Well, for goodness sake, you sure dig up the most interesting data. And I remember that sitting on the very front row was Larry MacPhail, who was running the Dodgers, and I thought he would just break all the buttons on his vest.

BOB: MacPhail figures in the third movement, the scherzo, in which MacPhail goes a-hunting for a star pitcher. He offers to trade Prospect Park and the Brooklyn Bridge even for Bob Feller, but the Cleveland management says no in the form of a big E-flat minor chord.

RED: Well, this is very intriguing. Robert Russell Bennett was not only a composer—he was conducting his own orchestra at that time on WOR and on the Mutual network—but also he was a marvelous orchestrator. To identify him better, he orchestrated *South Pacific*. And he was a baseball fan. He used to like to bring his grandson to Ebbets Field, and I would leave seats for them. And in narrating it, I was the voice in the fourth movement. And Robert Russell said over the air, he said, "Now, of course, Beethoven used a whole . . . chorus in his . . . symphony. But we're going to have to settle for Red Barber."

We finally located a recording of Bennett's symphony and played a bit of the fourth movement on the air. Accompanying Bennett's music is Red's description of a Dolph Camilli home run over Mel Ott's head. Brooklyn won the "game," 2–1, and I observed that this was odd since Bennett was a Giants fan. But Red pointed out that he, the Dodger announcer, had something to do with writing that script.

Red appreciated good music and good literature. John Bunzel of the Hoover Institution saw Red reading Arnold Toynbee on the beach at Chappaquiddick in 1960. Toynbee as a beach book? Bunzel also informed me of a couple of literary references in Red's play-by play:

> One afternoon he described a game in which the shortstop kicked away two ground balls before making a good play on a third—at which Red declared, "Like the Ancient Mariner, he stoppeth one of three!" (Here is the beginning of Coleridge's poem: "It is an ancient mariner/And he stoppeth one of three./ By the long gray beard and glittering eye,/ Now wherefore stopp'st thou me?" The Mariner has stopped one of three men going to a wedding.)
>
> On another occasion, a Dodger leadoff man hit a double and then remained rooted there while the next three batters grounded out, unable even to advance him to third. At which Red intoned, "They left him languishing there like the Prisoner of Chillon!" Now there was a more arcane reference, though Byron's "Sonnet on Chillon" and "Prisoner of Chillon" were also read in high schools.

Red Barber made genuine contributions to the language. Etymologists loved him, and some dictionaries still cite him as a reference source. A distant relative of the poet Sidney Lanier, Red loved the printed and spoken word. He expanded and celebrated the language, and left it enriched as a result.

"Rhubarb," for example, was Red's word for an argument. He called Ebbets Field "the rhubarb patch" because there were so many arguments there. If two great rivals were about to meet, he would predict, "There'll be blood on the moon." If a team was getting a bunch of hits, he would say they were "tearin' up the pea patch." Other announcers might say a lopsided game was "in the bag."

Red was more specific: he would have it "tied up in a croker sack." On the other hand, a close game might be "tighter than a new pair of shoes on a rainy day." A graceful infielder could be "movin' easy as a bank of fog," but watch out for that pitcher "wild as a hungry chicken hawk on a frosty morning." Pitchers might not be good hitters, but Freddie Fitzsimmons was "no slouch with the willow." A ball hit back to the pitcher would get a "come back little Sheba." If there was trouble fielding the ball, it might be because the ball was "slicker than oiled okra." Billy Cox had an arm so strong "he could toss a lamb chop past a hungry wolf." A runner employing a strategic slide "swung the gate" on the fielder trying to make the tag. "That was a wild game with the Cardinals last week—ooh, that one was full of fleas." After a home run, Tommy Henrich had a grin "big as a slice of watermelon." And look at Big Johnny Mize, who "swings that big bat as if it weighed no more than a dried turkey feather." When Jackie Robinson shook hands with Joe Louis, "photographers sprang up around them like rain lilies after a cloudburst."

Kenneth Kattzner, a *Morning Edition* listener in Washington, D.C., sent me some more. A high-scoring game had "developed into a ring-tailed, double-jointed doozy." "There's no action in the Dodger bullpen yet, but they're beginning to wiggle their toes a little." "This situation is as ticklish as the moment just before you are about to sneeze."

In April of 1982, listener Ken Pearson wrote from Brockton, Massachusetts, asking that Red explain something he said after the fourth game of the 1947 World Series. This was the game in which Yankee pitcher Bill Bevens took a no-hitter into the ninth inning, only to lose the game by giving up a double to Dodger pinch hitter Cookie Lavagetto.

RED: . . . I just sort of caught my breath and without thinking about it, Bob, I said, "Well, I'll be a suck-egg mule." Ed Murrow was then in charge of news and special events for CBS, and he was my superior there. He had hired me to be director of sports following Ted Husing. And he said to me later . . . , "You know, I think that is the perfect way to use rhetorical emphasis." And he had me come on his news program that night and explain it. And, Bob, I don't know how to explain it except that when you are doing something such as you and I are doing, live radio without any preparation, no script, you are just concentrating on the event, concentrating on your work, and something just comes out. In fact, later in that series, when DiMaggio hit what looked like a home run and Gionfriddo caught it against the left-center-field bullpen gate, I said, "Oh, doctor." And people have remembered that. And I hadn't planned it. It just came out.

That's what you do in ad-lib broadcasting. When you realize that, things just suddenly come out of your subconscious. . . . When you're talking in front of an open microphone, it sometimes frightens you. I know that that's one of the reasons many, many years ago, when I started broadcasting, I made a resolution that I would never say a word in private, a profane word or a foul word, that I could never say on a microphone, because I didn't want any speech habits to get to where maybe sometime, in an unguarded moment, I might say something.

Some of Red's expressions have become clichés now—"high on the hog," "walkin' in tall cotton," "liftin' the oxcart out of the ditch," "scraping around the bottom of the pickle barrel," "hollerin' down the rain barrel." Sammy Kaye would grouse during rehearsal "as cross as a bear with a boil in his nose." When the sponsor's executives visited the show, the ad agency men "would swarm around them like bees on a busted sugar barrel." Red seemed to have an endless supply, and he came by them honestly. His father was a storyteller with a great sense of humor. His mother was an English teacher who wouldn't let her children use bad grammar. They were the perfect parents to produce a well-read man who could tell funny stories with perfect grammar. Red felt his principal job was to report the truth, but he also knew he should be entertaining. The man who nearly joined a minstrel show had a flair for show biz.

And Red himself became part of English literature when he was featured in a James Thurber short story published in *The New Yorker.* The title of the story, "The Catbird Seat," was Red's most famous phrase, an expression he often used on the air. Red first heard the term at a penny-ante poker game in Cincinnati during the Depression. Red kept raising the bet, not knowing that another player, Frank Koch, was holding a pair of aces. Raking in the pot, Koch announced he had been "in the catbird seat all the while," and he thanked Red for making all those raises. Red said he was entitled to use the expression because he had paid for it. So when a baseball team had a comfortable lead, Red would say the team was "sittin' in the catbird seat."

In the Thurber story, a character uses many of Red's expressions, and Thurber wrote that the character picked them up by listening to Red Barber on the radio. Through this character, one master storyteller paid tribute to another. But the story of the story doesn't end there. Here's how Red told the tale during an NPR talk show on April 4, 1990:

> RED: . . . when I came to New York and started using those expressions over the radio, James Thurber would listen. And then he got the idea of doing "The Catbird Seat" for *The New Yorker* magazine. I had never met Mr. Thurber, and he never called and asked permission or anything else. And then a couple of years after that, I wanted to write a column for the *New York Journal American* . . . and I found out that I

couldn't use the title "The Catbird Seat." And also I saw in *Variety* that they were going to make a motion picture out of "The Catbird Seat," and I sent word to Mr. Thurber that that was gettin' the goose a little far from the gander. I understand that he got furious, and he had said he wanted to meet me sometime. And after I had remonstrated about his use of my language, he got mad. My daughter teaches English at LaGuardia Community College in New York. From time to time that story has come up and she's had certain students say to her, "Miss Barber, shouldn't your father be ashamed to steal that material from Thurber?" . . . When H. Allen Smith decided to write a book about a cat that owned a ball club and was going to name that cat Rhubarb, at least H. Allen called and asked, "Do you mind if I use that word 'rhubarb'?" I said, "Of course not, I'd be very pleased." But I never heard from Thurber.

It's a wonder that Thurber never wrote "The Saga of the Suck-Egg Mule."

Red Barber at station WLW in Cincinnati in 1937.

Dots and Dashes

UNTIL THE END OF WORLD WAR II, baseball announcers seldom traveled with the teams. Road games were done as re-creations with information supplied by Western Union, which had equipment at every ballpark. Some of the announcers doing re-creations went a bit overboard in trying to create the illusion that they actually were at the ballpark. They would use sound effects for crowd noise, vendors' calls and the crack of the bat. But Red was no con artist.

During the 1991 World Series, Red and I did a call-in show. When we got a call about doing road games in the old days, Red explained the operation of the service known as Western Union Paragraph One.

RED: At each of the sixteen ballparks, they had an experienced sending operator . . . and it was a service to anybody who wanted to buy it. I think it was twenty-five dollars. Bars would buy it. Clubs would buy it. Radio stations bought it. . . . This operator would send, and you would have a receiving operator in the studio with you. [The message would say,] "Lombardi up," and then would come "S1C," strike one called. "S2F," strike two fouled. "B1L," ball one low. Then "Out, fly to center." And then the next fellow up, "Goodman up." And that was the skeleton report that you got. As the announcer in the studio, you had to see that game in your mind's eye, and you had to fill it in. For example, in my case, I would say, "Lombardi's up. The big right-handed batter. He's got an open stance. He's got an interlocking finger grip. He's the only fellow in the big leagues who uses an interlocking finger grip. He broke the index finger on his left hand some years ago and, to protect it, began to interlock it in the lower two fingers of his right hand. And he's continued to hit that way. There he is, and he takes a strike. Strike one called. And now he leans down and gets a handful of dust and throws it away." You had to "photograph" all of the ballplayers so that you knew what they were doing. In other words, in my mind's eye, I saw it. Lombardi, after every pitch, always went down and got a handful of dirt and threw it away. So it wasn't that you were imagining things, at least not in my case. . . . As I used to explain it, you do a "live" game with your eyes, you did an out-of-town game with your mind.

BOB: But you didn't do anything with sound effects, crowd noise or anything like that?

RED: I never put in any sound noise, except I wanted the sound of the Western Union dots and dashes heard, and the typewriter sound that the receiving operator was using heard, because I wanted the audience to know that I was doing a Western Union re-creation, that I was not seeing this game for myself. I was very strong at that point. And the audience all over the years, I think they appreciated it. And when the wire would go out, as it would sometimes, I didn't have egg on my face.

President Reagan, you know, broadcast from Western Union reports out in Des Moines of the Chicago games. And he told with great glee about how he . . . made believe he was seeing the game, and how the wire went out and stayed out for . . . a dozen minutes or so. And he had a dog running across the field. He had a fight in the stands. He had a batter foul off eighteen or nineteen pitches. And then when the wire came back in, the first thing was "Pop to short."

Reagan liked to tell that story. In my case, I wanted the audience to know exactly what I was doing and that I was not seeing the game. And when the wire went out, I'm lazy. I just said, "Well, friends, the wire's gone out. We'll fill you in on the other games, bring you up to date." And if the wire was still out, I'd say, "Well, we'll just play some easy-to-listen-to music, and when the wire comes back in, we'll join you again."

Red was still the Cincinnati announcer when, in 1938, Reds pitcher Johnny Vander Meer became the only man to pitch consecutive no-hitters. The first one was an afternoon game in Cincinnati against the Boston Braves. The Braves announcers only did home games, so Red was the only broadcaster that day. Vander Meer's second no-hitter was on the road. It was the first night game ever played at Ebbets Field. There was no broadcast of that game because, by mutual agreement of the three New York teams, there were no broadcasts of any Yankee, Giant or Dodger home games. The announcers for visiting teams weren't even allowed to do wire service re-creations of games played in New York. But when the Associated Press sent the bulletin from Brooklyn that Vander Meer had made history, it seemed to Red that every German beer garden in Cincinnati was filled with Reds fans, and every last one of them wanted to call Red Barber's house and talk to him about it. He said the calls kept coming all night. From the next day on, Red's phone number was listed under the name of his wife, Lylah.

Two years later, Red was a Brooklyn announcer doing a Western Union re-creation of a Dodgers road game in Cincinnati. The Brooklyn pitcher was Tex Carleton.

> RED: The Dodgers opened up that season winning nine straight, and Carleton's no-hitter at Cincinnati was number nine . . . and Western Union would send a pilot word like "Hit," "Out," "Error," et cetera. Well, Carleton got two men out in the ninth inning and, of course, the story was, would he get the no-hitter? And the pilot word came, "Out," and I didn't wait for the details. I just said to the audience, "It's a no-hitter, I don't know how he's done it, but it's a no-hitter."

In other words, Red deliberately decided not to milk the suspense. He knew what the audience wanted to hear. He knew that it mattered less how Carleton got the last man out; the important fact was that Carleton had thrown a no-hitter. Red Barber was not going to "bury the lead," not even for a few seconds.

When Red died, I received a letter from Harry L. Moorman, who was then ninety years old. The letter began:

I was Red Barber's first telegrapher, receiving the out-of-town games by Morse code telegraph. A Western Union operator at the game described it by Morse code, and received a whole nickel an hour over his regular salary, and would have done it free as they all loved the dear old game.

He said one of his daughters was born at the same hour on the same day as Red's daughter, Sarah. He regretted having to leave Red for a better-paying job at *The Cincinnati Enquirer*, but those were the Great Depression years. After some highly complimentary remarks about Red and *Morning Edition*, he signed off with "73," explaining that "73" means "Best regards" among Morse operators.

John Kiesewetter, the radio and TV columnist for *The Cincinnati Enquirer*, interviewed Harry Moorman in 1991 and Red Barber in 1992. Moorman and Barber recalled having to do the Western Union re-creations in a room where, in summer, the temperature would be over a hundred degrees. Red recalled Moorman collapsing over his Teletype machine one day, though he quickly straightened up. Moorman told Kiesewetter about a re-creation on July 21, 1934. The temperature outside was 109 degrees.

It got so hot, Red took his shirt off. Perspiration was coming off my ears, my fingers and my nose. And Red took his undershirt off. And here the door opens, and Mr. Crosley [the owner of the Reds and the radio station] in a full suit and a stiff collar and tie, and [he] had two dowagers come in, and they saw the bare chest and were ready to scream, and ran out again. And the next day I asked Red, "Were you criticized for being bare-chested?" And Red said, "No, nobody said a thing." It was miserable. My pants were soaked, just like I'd been swimming. Nobody brought us a Coke or a glass of water or anything. This was up in the sixth-floor storeroom, where they moved the wire.

I wonder how Ronald Reagan would have handled that one.

Station Identification

Years ago, an NPR producer, making the case for the regular turnover of commentators, said he didn't want our programs to resemble the op-ed pages of a lot of newspapers—filled with the opinions of people who said everything they had to say years ago but continue to say it. Red Barber told the same stories for years and people loved hearing them again and again. The stories were good and the storyteller was even better. He turned the routine into theater, using his childhood interest in show business to good advantage and bringing every available prop onto the stage—just as during his play-by-play career he filled rain delays by describing the work of the grounds crew as they covered the infield with a tarpaulin. Listeners stayed with the broadcasts and "watched" the grounds crew working on the radio.

I think the early radio broadcasters—the good ones, such as Red, Arthur Godfrey, Lowell Thomas and Edward R. Murrow—owed a lot to theater, vaudeville, the tent shows and the public speaking forums that were once part of America. They knew how to tell a story, how to modulate their voices, when to slow down, when to pause and how to deliver a punch line. With a few well-chosen words effectively delivered they could illuminate, motivate and inspire. They were so good at it that they had us filling in the blanks for ourselves.

Red Barber brought to NPR a kind of presence that none of us had. It's an intangible thing that doesn't lend itself to easy definition. Other *Morning Edition* sports commentators had gifts Red didn't possess, but not the same magic. Red did not have Bill Littlefield's writing talent or Frank Deford's zest for tackling controversial issues. Red didn't have the insider's perspective that Mark Murphy and now Tim Green articulate so well. John Feinstein was even dippier about his cat, Chutzpah, than Red was about his cat Arwe, but Feinstein could never get away with doing animal stories the way Red did.

The NPR that Red joined in 1981 was far different from the NPR of today. It was still establishing its identity as a news organization. Some years earlier, one of my first NPR producers kept telling me that *All Things Considered* was not a news program, it was a magazine of the air. Features were plentiful, along with storytelling. We couldn't afford a lot of thorough reporting, and the news we delivered followed a broad definition of what constituted news. Three network presidents and four news directors later, the budget is bigger, the staff is deeper, the standards are higher, the focus is more narrow and the audience is growing. We take ourselves more seriously than we did before. In 1981 Red's stories were "very NPR," while in 1992 they contrasted sharply with the rest of our programming. Red's popularity thrived anyway, and I'm certain that if he could return a hundred years from now he would adapt to whatever kind of radio exists then—or, perhaps more accurately, whatever kind of radio exists then would adapt to and accommodate *him*.

Jay Kernis was the senior producer of *Morning Edition* when Red joined the program. He says Red "got" NPR, meaning Red understood that we were a group of people committed to radio as something more than a jukebox or a cash register. Most NPR commentators sign on to gain access to our audience, which includes many highly influential people. But Kernis thinks Red had a different motive. NPR was the only national radio outlet that would let him tell a story. The term "sound bite" still is not in our vocabulary.

No one dared to tell Red Barber that our audience didn't want to hear about the flora and fauna of Tallahassee. It's a good thing we didn't, because we would have been absolutely wrong. People loved hearing about these subjects and Red knew that from the start. Sure, talking about them was part of his act, but listeners trusted him to be an honest reporter on plants, animals *and* sports. Ultimately, our subject was life itself. Producer Mark Schramm and newscaster Carl Kasell believe Red's humanity was the draw for listeners. Schramm says Red was unpretentious, and that had great appeal to a radio audience accustomed to hearing the boasts of those with lesser gifts. Kasell, who often filled in for me in the early years, cites Red's interest in music, literature, theater and, of course, nature. Listeners knew Red was not a one-dimensional man. He was never just a sports personality, but one who enjoyed a broad range of interests. Jay Kernis says the listeners regarded Red as the wise old granddad who wouldn't embarrass us in front of our friends at a party.

And who was I for those four minutes? When I talked with Red Barber, he wouldn't allow me to be Bob Edwards, the cool, calm *Morning Edition* host. Kernis says that when I talked with Red, listeners heard the lifting of the journalist's detachment and skepticism, even my normal curiosity. Instead, listeners heard my reverence and respect. They heard a human being, not an anchorman. They heard the Colonel, Red's straight man, who, in the early years, was just hanging on and hoping to survive the broadcast, and at the end was finding ways to help Red do his best work.

Morning radio listeners want both predictability and spontaneity. That's not a contradiction, and Red was the perfect illustration of the point. Red was predictable in that he was on *Morning Edition* every Friday morning at

7:35 eastern time. Everything else was spontaneous. There was no telling what he was going to say or how I was going to react to it. I suspect that the attraction for some listeners was to hear me squirm when Red put me on the spot. That was okay with me as long as it was bringing new listeners to the program. In time, the listeners heard something else: they heard two radio men, born nearly forty years apart, becoming friends. For one, this represented the highlight of a career. For the other, it was a triumphant final chapter.

Red with Leo Durocher at Brooklyn's Ebbets Field in 1939, Red's first year in Brooklyn and Leo's first year as a manager. Leo was also the Dodger shortstop.

Brooklyn

RED BARBER'S LAST SEASON in Cincinnati was 1938. By then, the Reds' general manager, Larry MacPhail, had had what was politely called a "falling out" with principal owner Powel Crosley and had moved on to Brooklyn. One of MacPhail's first decisions in Brooklyn was to broadcast the Dodgers' games. This meant breaking the agreement among the New York teams not to broadcast.

Brooklyn had been a party to that agreement, but MacPhail had not. MacPhail got General Mills to sponsor the games and station WOR to carry the broadcasts. He also had an announcer in mind, but the General Mills people asked MacPhail not to tell Red that he was to get the job for fear that Red would rob the Wheaties treasury. MacPhail agreed. The cereal maker told Red he was to broadcast games for one of the New York teams. It didn't tell him which one. So Red went to work for General Mills for a mere eight thousand dollars. Powel Crosley offered him sixteen thousand dollars to stay in Cincinnati, but Red, fearing his chance at the big time might never come again, was bound for New York. Once the agreement was made, Red learned he was to do the Dodger games over station WOR.

The Giants were not pleased. Giants road secretary Eddie Brannick told MacPhail that he too would sign a contract with a fifty-thousand-watt radio station and blast the Dodger broadcasts into the river. MacPhail, always pugnacious after a few drinks, relayed the news to his announcer. Here's how Red described it in his book *The Broadcasters*:

> MacPhail was now a wild man, redder than a bleeding beet. He paused just long enough to refill his lungs, and he bellowed again . . . and by now he was jabbing me with his right index finger.
>
> "By God . . . he threatened me . . . threatened to blast me into the river. . . . Listen—I don't know what announcer they've got, or what fifty-thousand-watt radio station . . . but I've got WOR, and THAT is a fifty-thousand-watt radio station." He jabbed me so deep I've still got the hole in my chest. "And . . . I've got you. . . . Now, young man, here are my instructions—I-don't-want-to-be-blasted-into-the-river."

The Giants joined with the Yankees to battle MacPhail's Dodgers on radio. The Giants and Yankees were never at home at the same time, so the teams announced that the home games of both clubs would be broadcast and the announcer for all games would be Arch McDonald, who had been the Washington Senators broadcaster.

Time magazine, in its issue dated April 17, 1939, carried

a lengthy story about the plans for Giant and Yankee broadcasts. The story was particularly flattering to Mc-Donald, praising his great skill. The article mentioned nothing about Brooklyn and Red Barber. Red called it the ultimate insult—to be ignored.

Later, he said that *Time* had done him a favor: it gave him incentive. "If I needed anything," he wrote, "to make me completely at one with three million Brooklynites who hated and resented New York and Manhattan and the Giants and the Yankees, this complete rebuff was it. My reaction was pure Brooklyn: 'Oh yeah? I'll show 'em.' " Red "showed 'em" by doing something special for the first broadcast: he got WOR to give him some extra time before the game, during which he interviewed Giants manager Bill Terry and the Dodgers' Leo Durocher, who was managing his first game. Pre-game shows are routine today, but not in 1939. Red made sure it was *his* broadcast the New York–area baseball fans were talking about the next day.

There must have been a stunning collision of accents. Red Barber, born in Mississippi and reared in Florida, was broadcasting to an audience whose ears were used to the vowels and consonants of Flatbush and Canarsie. The clash probably required a period of adjustment for both Red and his listeners. But there was no question about the final result. Dodger fans were drawn to the Ol' Redhead and his Dixie metaphors. And Red was conscious of the place the Dodgers held in Brooklyn hearts. He knew that Brooklyn resented being the butt of so many jokes. Brooklyn never wanted to be part of New York City in the first place, and yet it was treated as Manhattan's stepchild. As long as Brooklyn had the Dodgers, Brooklyn had an identity.

In his book *Bums*, Peter Golenbock writes:

> You could walk through the streets of Brooklyn and follow the play-by-play of the Dodger game going from your house down into the subway or wherever you were going.

Everyone had a radio, and all those radios were tuned to the Dodger game as it was being described by Walter "Red" Barber. It was a prevailing sound of the street. Many fans built their entire lives around the Dodgers. For some, a whole summer was based on the team, and wherever people gathered in Brooklyn, at game time there would be a radio. On the boardwalk, in the cars, on the trolleys. During the summer, all anyone talked about was the Dodgers, and the only station tuned in during the afternoon was the Dodger station. If the Dodgers were a religion, then Red Barber was Billy Graham.

As the voice of the Dodgers, Red Barber was the voice of Brooklyn. Mel Allen told me, "Red *made* Brooklyn." Ebbets Field became the place to be, and fans flocked to the ballpark.

Ebbets Field in Brooklyn at the time of Red Barber's broadcasts has been the subject of plays, movies, TV series and books. It was an old bandbox of a park, but the fans were so close to the action they could hear the infield chatter and see the facial expressions of their heroes as they went about their work. Here's how the Ol' Redhead described it during a 1950 game:

For those of you who haven't seen Ebbets Field, it's a double-decked stadium, and the double-decking begins at right field's corner. In other words, there is no stand in back of right field. That's the famous fence or wall, the right-field wall. But the stands go all the way around in a rough U. Campanella fouls this one back. In back of right field is Bedford Avenue. Curveball, outside, ball two. That's one of the big thoroughfares, it's about a six-lane street in Brooklyn. But that's a forty-foot-high right-field wall. If you want to be exact, thirty-nine and a half feet—nineteen and a half feet of concrete and then twenty feet of wire panels. Pitch low, outside, ball three. The field is in wonderful shape, the ballpark looking just as pretty as a brand-new bug. Got a lot of baseball going today.

Our tape ended there, and I still don't know what Campy did with that 3–1 or 3–2 pitch.

Red's popularity in Brooklyn was so great that the Democratic party asked him to run for the U.S. House of Representatives from Brooklyn. He was told that his victory was assured and that he would not have to campaign. Red declined the offer. Recalling the incident for an interviewer many years later, Red said he told the Democrats, "I'm not getting into that league."

Brooklyn-born writer Alan Lelchuk wrote a novel titled *Brooklyn Boy* in which young Aaron Schlossberg knows that "Red Barber was as important to both kids and grown-ups as, say, General Eisenhower or President Roosevelt."

> He was the Voice of the Bums, and the voice—maybe conscience—of the borough. It was a measure of Brooklyn's hospitality and worldliness that Aaron and friends had adopted this Mississippi-born, Southern-accented gentleman to speak for them, sing to them. When Red was on the air, telling us about Pistol Pete crashing into the wall yet again or about Fireman Casey coming in from the bull pen to put out another fire, you could hear his special phrases everywhere you went, on the beaches or front stoops, in drugstores or candy stores, in parlors or barbershops, at lunch wagons or pool halls, from car radios, portables, or consoles. He was soft-spoken, scrupulous, knowledgeable, rhythmic, humorous, down-home, eloquent. Always eloquent. His voice filled the streets, shops, seasides of the borough, surrounded and suffused us with its sweetness and moral light; a very different voice from that older Brooklyn singer, Walt Whitman.

Lelchuk says of his young protagonist: "He didn't just go to the ball games with Mr. Barber to learn about line drives, curveballs and outfield play; he learned just as much about farm life and history and geography. Without Aaron's quite knowing it, Red was his earliest teacher."

Steve Gorlick was a Dodger fan as a child, but he never

saw Ebbets Field. Gorlick is from Los Angeles and his actor father took him to the first Dodger games in the Los Angeles Coliseum. But today Gorlick is a college administrator who lives in Brooklyn, just five blocks from where Ebbets Field once stood. On Friday mornings, he would time his morning run so that he would be at the site of Ebbets Field at 7:35 when I would be talking with Red on *Morning Edition*. For some time he thought he was standing near center field, but one of the locals eventually told him that he was at home plate. The important point is that Gorlick wanted to honor a time, a place and a man special to his neighbors. Red Barber had moved to a national stage, but he would always belong to Brooklyn.

Red at Crosley Field in Cincinnati in 1934, his first major league baseball season.

Play-by-Play

TERRY CASHMAN, THE PROLIFIC WRITER of baseball songs, has a number that goes, "Play-by-play—I saw it on the radio." Cashman knows that the good ones can make you see the action.

Hearing tapes of Red, I see the players when he sets the defense. His description of Ebbets Field gives me a mental picture of a stadium that I never actually saw with my eyes and never will. When Red says that he and Connie Desmond and Vin Scully "will be back here tomorrow at the same old stand," I see them in the booth and feel the heat of a summer afternoon at the conclusion of a ball game. Red painted pictures more real than the work of any portrait artist. Here he is describing the 1936 World Series:

> Dick Bartell up, and this is a tight ball game and certainly a splendid exhibition of what a World Series ball game should be. Hadley winds up. Delivers. . . . Bartell takes inside on the letters for ball one. The first pitch of the fourth inning. Bartell stands there with his forward left foot right up against the plate, his right foot crouched underneath him. The pitch. Dick swings. . . . It's a high foul behind third. Rolfe is underneath it in the coach's box, waiting, and squeezes it for the out. And Rolfe, after he caught that foul behind third base, shook his head very wryly as though to wring tears out of his eyes. The sky overhead is a very beautiful robin's-egg blue with, as the boys say, very few angels in the form of clouds in it. It's a very tough sky for the players to look into. And left field at Yankee Stadium is the sun garden.

How can you *not* see that sky?

Sometimes Red didn't need the gift of gab to paint pictures. He did it simply by passing on little details of the scene. A bit later in that same game he said that a player "went down to second base, quite a bit faster than the 'elevated' whistling behind right and right-center field this afternoon." Now the listener could put a train behind the outfield wall. It's a nice touch, and it didn't take a Rembrandt to fill that space on the canvas, just someone with enough smarts to pass on a visual reference point that might not have occurred to another announcer caught up in the action on the field. One of my childhood heroes was Claude Sullivan, who broadcast Cincinnati Reds baseball and University of Kentucky football and basketball in my part of the country. Sullivan began every broadcast with a description of the place where the game was being played. By the time he finished, I could smell decades of sweat in the ancient fieldhouses of the Southeastern Conference.

Red Barber had the added gift of the folksy expressions described earlier. If Marty Marion or Billy Herman was "movin' easy as a bank of fog," one got a picture of the waiting infielder trying to anticipate the play. When an Ernie Lombardi or a Johnny Mize was batting, the listener got a sense of the power of these men and concluded the pitcher had better be careful because either was capable of smashing the next pitch out of the park. We saw Joe DiMaggio up close to the plate, challenging the pitcher. We saw Don Newcombe bearing down, daring the hitter not to back away from the next high hard one.

This is the drama of the game. This is real. These confrontations are taking place, and a great sportswriter can help his reader become part of the experience by carefully choosing the right words to describe a player rising to the occasion or choking under the pressure. But a broadcaster cannot carefully choose his words after the fact. The broadcaster is describing the action as it is happening and must use the words that pop into his mind. There are no second chances. A player hits a ball. Another player fields the ball and throws to still another player who tags a fourth player. Who were those guys? The broadcaster has to know all the names immediately and describe what they're doing, how they're doing it and what the consequences are. It doesn't happen in slow motion; it's *bang-bang-bang*. Try it sometime. And while you're writing the play down in your scorebook, don't forget that the sponsor wants you to plug the product, the ball club wants you to promote next week's helmet night, the local stations would like a station break soon, the FCC expects an ID at this moment and you promised the boss you'd wish a happy birthday to his sister in Moline. The team owner wants you to sound more animated, the newspaper critic thinks you should be more journalistic, your family urges you to be more personable and common sense tells you to be yourself. It's a wonder that more play-by-play announcers don't give up and try doing TV game shows or radio talk shows.

When Red Barber began in radio, he tried to imitate someone else. So did I. Maybe everyone in the business does that at the beginning. We can't sound like ourselves because we don't yet know who we are, at least in radio terms. At WRUF in Gainesville in 1930, Red called himself Walter Barber and imitated Milton Cross, who did the Metropolitan Opera broadcasts. He also tried to sound like his hero, Graham McNamee. That was a big mistake. There already was a Graham McNamee. Who needed another? Had he continued, it would have been a tragedy, because we never would have had a Red Barber. No one ever has succeeded in broadcasting by trying to be someone other than himself or herself (Rich Little doesn't count). Red's first boss, Major Garland Powell, told Red to be confident of his own gifts and not try to steal from others. Thank you, Major Powell.

Among those gifts was the skill with language he learned from his mother. Author Neil Postman wrote, "My own language education began in a serious way with my attempts to imitate the sentence structure, vocabulary, metaphors and even cadence of two people: Red Barber and Franklin Delano Roosevelt." And Postman added that "it was from Red Barber that I first heard the words 'ignominy' and 'concomitant,' neither of which I use very much today but from which I learned that such words can be used to describe real and important events. . . ." I don't know the context in which Red used "ignominy," though one can see quite a bit of that in sports. I know exactly how he used "concomitant." I've heard a tape of Red calling a Yankee game in which Phil Rizzuto singled and the outfielder bobbled the ball. What did Rizzuto do next? He "took second on the concomitant error." That's precise usage. Red was not flaunting some obscure piece of knowledge; he was using the proper word to describe precisely what had taken place. If he sent his listeners to their dictionaries, that was fine with him.

Still another component of the painting of radio pictures is in the very technique of play-by-play. Red taught me a lesson that's so easy and so beneficial that you would think all play-by-play broadcasters would have picked it up by now. They haven't. On February 28, 1992, in one of the very few Friday talks that was planned and programmed, I asked Red whether a broadcaster uses spring training to retrain his eye to follow the ball.

RED: You follow the ball . . . at the moment it's hit. But then you pick up the defensive ballplayer, especially the outfielder. A lot of broadcasters make the mistake of trying to judge that a ball's going to go into the stands and then it gets caught by an outfielder and then they've got egg on their face. I always picked up the outfielder, and I understand you've got a couple of calls that I made in the World Series of 1947— which is a matter of broadcasting technique that I think might be interesting. First would be where the ball was going, then what the outfielder did, and then what happened.

BOB: Okay, we've got one from game four. This is where Bill Bevens has the no-hitter going for the Yankees into the ninth inning. And we got two out, bottom of the ninth. And Lavagetto's up.

RED (on tape): *Two out, last of the ninth. Two to one, New York. Well, Eddie Stanky stepping in. You know, Ewell Blackwell had pitched one no-hitter and was on the verge of pitching a second successive one against the Dodgers. He had gone eight and a third innings, and Stanky broke up Blackwell's bid for two straight no-hitters. So Stanky's up with the idea of trying to— Wait a minute! Stanky's being called back from the plate and Lavagetto goes up to hit! . . . Gionfriddo walks off second, Miksis off first. They're both ready to go on anything. Two men out, last of the ninth. The pitch. Swung on. There's a drive hit out toward the right-field corner.*

Henrich going back. He can't get it. It's off the wall for a base
hit. Here comes the tying run and here comes the winning
run.

BOB: Well, there were a lot of remarkable things about
that call, but indeed you were following Henrich.

RED: Well, you see, that's what I said. You pick up the
outfielder because the outfielder will tell you the ultimate destination of the ball. And if you noticed, I
picked up Henrich and said that he couldn't get it.

BOB: Here's another one. Game six, same World Series.
And it's the bottom of the sixth. Two men on. The
Dodgers are leading, 8–5.

RED (on tape): *Joe DiMaggio up, holding that club down at*
the end. Big fellow sets. Hatten pitches. A curveball, high
outside, for ball one. So the Dodgers are ahead, 8–5. And the
crowd well knows that with one swing of the bat this fellow is
capable of making it a brand-new game again. Joe leans in.
He is one for three today. Six hits so far in this series. Outfield
deep around toward left. The infield overshifted. Here's the
pitch. Swung on. Belted. It's a long one! Deep into left-
center. Back goes Gionfriddo, back, back, back, back, back,
back. He makes a one-handed catch against the bullpen. Oh,
doctor!

BOB: So the crowd was watching the ball—you were
watching Al Gionfriddo.

RED: Well, that's what I learned, Bob, when I first got to
the big leagues in 1934. Always go with the outfielder,
and he will tell you. And if the ball goes into the stands,
he will look up and watch it go into the stands with
you.

Red also knew when to shut up. After his call of a big
play, he would stop talking and let the crowd noise have
the microphone. The crowd and its reactions were part of
the story. After Bobby Thomson's home run in the 1951
National League playoff, Red let the crowd noise go for a
full minute. During this same time, Russ Hodges, doing

the Giant broadcast, was screaming "The Giants win the pennant!" over and over again. Red believed announcers sounded foolish trying to talk over the crowd noise. Besides, he could hurt his vocal cords doing that.

Mel Allen told me he used to tease Red about his famous egg timer, Red's reminder to give the score every three minutes. Working with Red one day, Mel noticed the sand had run through and Red had not given the score. But Mel said he didn't dare turn the thing over or even point to it. He waited until after the broadcast to joke that Red used it only as a prop or a gimmick.

On the day of a broadcast, Red made certain that he read the newspaper—*all* of the newspaper. He could not predict what would happen in a broadcast or what information he might need, but he was not going to sound ignorant on the air. He was not going to sound as though he didn't know what was going on in the world outside of sports.

He made mistakes. In fact, he made some whoppers. He once had the wrong man playing third base for the entire game. He apologized at the beginning of his next broadcast. The apology was important to his credibility. He didn't care for people who couldn't admit their mistakes. In his book *The Broadcasters,* he told the story of Bill Stern, who frequently misidentified the ballcarrier during college football games. Since this was radio, Stern could get away with having the ballcarrier lateral to the player who had actually carried the ball. Stern's games set records for laterals. But Stern was also a hypocrite; he could not admit his own mistakes but was quick to make fun of others who made errors. Stern had a lot of fun with Clem McCarthy, who once had the wrong horse winning the Preakness. When McCarthy heard that Stern was giving him the business, he said, "Well, you can't lateral a horse."

Red learned from his mistakes. He also learned from mistakes made by others. At one of Red's first games in the big leagues, the Cincinnati public-address man announced

a pitching change before being ordered to do so by the
umpire-in-chief, Bill Klem. Klem was furious and gave the
PA man a humiliating dressing-down that even Red could
hear up in the booth. This is how Red learned the rule
about when and how a player officially enters a game, and
it paid off several years later when he was doing a World
Series broadcast. The New York Giants brought in a relief
pitcher who was not the one announced by the PA man.
Red noticed immediately that it was the wrong pitcher and
told his listeners before the argument even began on the
field. And because he had discussed the rule with Bill Klem
after the 1934 incident in Cincinnati, Red knew that the
pitcher whose name had been announced would be required to pitch to one batter before the Giants could bring
in the pitcher they wanted. He must have sounded like a
baseball Einstein that day. But he simply had learned from
another man's mistake.

Broadcasting was Red's job. He had no patience for people who couldn't understand that. Some think broadcasting looks too much like fun to be real work, and in Red's
case the broadcasts had to do with men playing children's
games. He had to convince people that this was a career, a
profession, something that commanded respect. This was
difficult for Red because the public often saw his job being
done by ex-athletes with varying degrees of articulation
and literacy. Red hated that. It galled him that the position
he had worked so hard to achieve could be handed over to
an unappreciative jock simply because he once had the
ability to hit a baseball or throw a forward pass. The one
exception he made was for Pat Summerall, who has been
a broadcaster (and a good one) for so long that maybe
even he doesn't remember that he used to be a kicker for
the Giants.

Another problem with many among the new breed was
that they never shut up. Red said they came from "the
Gee-Whiz-Jack-Armstrong-All-American-Boy School of
Microphone Mouthings." He would remind these guys

that "not every pitch is a 'great' pitch. Not every effort on a two-yard gain is a 'great' effort." Having read this, I was shocked to hear that Red spoke well of Howard Cosell. Red believed that Cosell's act reflected what Cosell had to do in order to get noticed in a tough market.

Red did not endear himself to other broadcasters. He was demanding—a perfectionist. He did not suffer fools. He was candid, perhaps to a fault, though he didn't see it that way. He expected others to have the same professional approach to the job that he had. Ernie Harwell, Jim Woods and Vin Scully are frank about how difficult it was to work with Red, yet they all say they profited from the discipline. I once asked Chicago broadcaster Jack Brickhouse about Red, and his face contorted into a pretzel. It seemed to me there must have been some painful memories he didn't care to recall. Mel Allen told me nice things about Red, but I got the impression that doing so was an effort for him. I am not so mired in hero worship that I don't know why they felt that way about Red. We at NPR also got the treatment sometimes. But Red was no more demanding of anyone else than he was of himself. He got to where he was by being self-disciplined and by outhustling his peers. He delivered everything he promised and he expected others to do the same. There should be more like him in every position of responsibility.

It's fitting that Red gave one of his last long interviews to NBC's Bob Costas for the syndicated radio program *Costas Coast to Coast*. No doubt Red was impressed with the interviewer's preparation. Without the benefit of the six hundred Fridays I had with Red, Costas seemed to know just what to ask. I agree with the many people who regard Costas as the best interviewer and the best studio host in sports broadcasting today. Add his play-by-play talents and you have a triple-threat sportscaster. By all rights, he should be the heir to Red Barber's stature in sports broadcasting. But he can never be a Red Barber. No one can. And Red explained why to Bob Costas.

RED: I doubt very much that I could even get a foothold in radio or television today. When I began broadcasting at Cincinnati and at Brooklyn, I think there were three commercials for nine innings. So it meant you were on the air all afternoon. You had opportunity. You had room on the air to tell stories. Now, as you well know, you gotta hustle at the end of every third out. You're not allowed any talking time between innings. You're not allowed any feature time. If you're doing television today, you don't have an opportunity to tell a feature story. You don't have an opportunity really to be much of a personality. See, Graham McNamee was a great personality because he began broadcasting when there were no commercials at all. Ted Husing was a great personality. Bill Munday was a great personality. We had, you might say, air room to be a personality. I had a chance to be a beginning personality.

In other words, Costas, Al Michaels and the other fine young sportscasters are being cheated by the very success of sports on radio and TV, success established by those of Red Barber's generation. They're not the only ones being cheated. The loss is ours, too. Cartoon figures and the anonymous actors who star in commercials we see and hear between innings are more familiar to us than the people broadcasting the game. The winner of this contest is Madison Avenue. As a result, the broadcasters of today cannot become as much a part of their audiences' lives as Red did in his day. He accomplished it with a remarkable array of skills, all of which began with the simple ability to keep his eyes open and describe what he saw.

At work in the press box in Cincinnati.

No-Hitters

THE FIRST MAJOR LEAGUE GAME Red saw was the first major league game he broadcast—and it very nearly was the first major league no-hitter he ever witnessed. With one out in the last inning, Lon Warneke had a no-hitter going against the Reds. This was not a bulletin to the radio audience, because Red Barber had been telling them all along that the Reds were hitless. Red didn't know any better; it was his first big league game, and he didn't know there was a taboo against the broadcaster's mentioning that a potential no-hitter was in the making. The superstition has it that to speak of the no-hitter after the fifth inning is to jinx the pitcher. The mere mention of the term "no-hitter" is enough to break the spell—somehow the batters will be able to hit pitching they couldn't hit before the announcer spilled the beans.

Red pointed out that the taboo, in its original context, made some sense.

> This hoodoo business started in the dugouts with a fairly reasonable premise—a teammate would not mention a possible no-hitter for fear of putting undue pressure on his pitcher, who just might be pitching away blissfully unaware of what he was doing. Then, before radio came along, this hoodoo, or jinx, got up to the press box, and the writers turned silent whenever the occasion presented itself. When radio got going, the hoodoo spread into the broadcasting booths. Not mine.

People who are baseball fans are familiar with the game's superstitions. People who are not baseball fans may read this and wonder if they are misunderstanding something. Would grown men and women—fully mature people with some education in their backgrounds, people with enough facility with the language to be considered intelligent and articulate—be party to such a silly, childish exercise? After all, the pitcher can't know what the sportswriter is writing about him, and it's highly unlikely that he is going to hear what the broadcaster is saying about him. So this ballplayers' superstition cannot be perpetuated by writers and broadcasters, can it? Well, yes, it can. And the taboo is observed to this day by some of the best-known broadcasters in sports. Some will dance around it; they'll say pitcher X "really is shutting them down today," or "there's not much happening for the visiting team's batters today." What they *won't* say is that pitcher X has a no-hitter going.

Imagine you're a reporter covering D-Day. Ike has given you all the details and told you to report anything you want except the fact that Allied troops have landed in France and the invasion of Nazi-occupied Europe is under way. Well now, that's going to be a curious story, isn't it? In the case of a no-hitter, the broadcaster is imposing self-censorship. What kind of reporter ignores the lead on the best story he's going to have for quite a while? No reporter does, which is why Red always told his listeners when a no-hitter was in the making.

On opening day in 1934, with one out in the ninth inning, Adam Comorosky singled right past Warneke. If he had reacted faster, Warneke might have preserved his own no-hitter. Was it Red Barber's fault? Did Comorosky get enough wood on that ball because Red had blabbed about Cincinnati having no hits? Of course not, but you can bet Red caught some flak in the Cubbies' locker room.

Red was determined to buck this thing. He was a reporter and he wasn't going to be part of some silly superstition. But in recalling what may have been the most exciting game he ever broadcast—Bill Bevens's near no-hitter in the 1947 World Series—he seemed to waver, if only for a second. Red was working the game with Mel Allen. What was different about this game was that it was the World Series, not a local broadcast. Red's work was being heard around the world. The pressure was brutal. And everyone listening knew the taboo.

> Allen was of the hoodoo school, one of its staunch members. There would have been no question at all had he had the mike. Allen would have cut his throat before he'd state that Bevens had given no hits. . . . When I leaned into the mike . . . and said that Bevens had given one run, so many walks and no hits, the breath gurgled in Allen's throat like a country boy trying to swallow a chinaberry seed.

What happened to Bevens was worse than what happened to Warneke. Pinch hitter Cookie Lavagetto doubled in the tying and winning runs. Bevens not only blew his no-hitter and a place in history, he lost a World Series game on a single pitch. Was it the Barber curse again?

> . . . there was much nastiness that night in New York about what I had done, especially from so-called Yankee fans. I was even criticized on the radio by a couple of local announcers. I was held up that night as the man who had done the most unsportsmanlike thing ever in the history of sports announcing.

Bevens knew better. He had walked two men before Lavagetto was brought in to pinch-hit. The walks did him in. A pitcher doesn't put the tying and winning runs on base in the ninth inning and give his opponents such a golden opportunity.

Red never jinxed a pitcher. He broadcast plenty of no-hitters. There was Tex Carleton's hitless game re-created by Teletype. Red worked the first of Johnny Vander Meer's back-to-back no-hitters. He broadcast Rex Barney's no-hitter in 1948. And though Red Barber has come and gone, the taboo continues.

Red interviewing Leo Durocher before the first major league game ever televised, August 26, 1939.

TV Pioneer

RED OFTEN SAID THAT HE WAS at the right place at the right time. He wasn't just being modest. In broadcasting, as in many careers, timing is everything. I found NPR when both the network and I were young and inexperienced. It's tougher to make the team today. Radio as a popular medium of information and entertainment was less than a decade old when Red broadcast his first program. Television was yet to come, and when it did, Red was there.

TV was demonstrated to the public for the first time at the 1939 World's Fair in New York. That also happened to be Red's first season at Brooklyn. In May, an experimental NBC TV station carried a baseball game between Columbia and Princeton. The announcer was Bill Stern.

RED: Several months later, . . . Doc Morton, who was in charge of this infant called television for NBC—he and I had had an acquaintance over the years—asked me to come by his office, and I did. And he said, "You know, we've done this game up at Columbia, but I'm dying to do a big league baseball game. And I know there's no reason to contact the Giants or the Yankees because they're so anti-radio, they would certainly be anti-television. I don't know MacPhail, but you do and you're working for him. Would you ask Larry MacPhail if he would let us, let NBC, televise one baseball game, any one that he selects?" So I went into MacPhail's office. And you remember MacPhail was quite a pioneer. He had pioneered flying a ball club, pioneered night baseball, pioneered radio. So I said, "Larry, would you like another first?" And he said, "Yeah, what is it?" I said, "Televise a ball game." So he got in touch with Doc Morton and they agreed to do the first game of a Saturday afternoon doubleheader, which was at Ebbets Field, August the twenty-sixth, 1939.

The Cincinnati Reds were in with Bucky Walters and Paul Derringer and company. The Reds were on their way to a pennant. It was a big day. And MacPhail said to Morton, "However, for letting you televise this ball game, I want something." Morton said, "What is it?" MacPhail said, "I want you to install a television receiving set in the pressroom, so the directors of the ball club, and myself and the writers, can see the telecast." At that time, Bob, I don't think there were a hundred receiving sets in creation. So that was the first fee that television paid to sports. And I remember that I announced the ball game, and that's how that came about.

BOB: Were you nervous?

RED: Oh, I don't think so, Bob, any more than are you nervous any morning when you get up and go to work?

BOB: Every one of them.

RED: Well, I think all professionals have, should we say, an anticipatory preparation. But you're not really nervous, otherwise you couldn't do the work day after day.

BOB: We found . . . an NBC still photo from that day. You're interviewing Leo Durocher.

RED: Well, I interviewed Leo Durocher, I interviewed Bill McKechnie—the Reds' manager—Dolph Camilli, Bucky Walters. There were quite a few. And it was a very historic day. And that was the day, August the twenty-sixth, 1939, that set it all in motion.

Later in 1939, Red would do play-by-play of the first football games ever televised. But this August baseball game included another important TV first. It was Red Barber who did the first TV commercials. Oh, doctor!

BOB: Now, according to the advertising museum in Portland [Oregon], there were no scripts, cue cards or rehearsals for the commercials. How did you do them?

RED: They had two cameras. Of course, it was black and white. There was no monitor in those days. There was no assistant director, et cetera. And we had three radio sponsors: Ivory soap, Mobil gas and Wheaties. So, of course, there were no rehearsals. Nobody ever thought about a thing like that. So when the time came to do one for Socony-Vacuum, I just put on a

filling station cap, held up a can of oil and ad-libbed a
little bit. Did the same thing for a bar of Ivory soap.
Poured some Wheaties in a bowl, sliced a banana, put
some milk on it and said, "This is the breakfast of
champions." And so that was not only the first telecast
of a sporting event in the big leagues, it was the first
time commercials were on, and nobody got any
money.

BOB: You were seated among the fans.

RED: Yes. One camera was down on the ground level
behind home plate. The other one was on the upper
stands in back of third base, right out with the fans,
and I was sittin' right there with 'em. And I guarantee
you I had hundreds of helpers.

BOB: So now we know who to blame for putting commercials on television.

RED: That's right, and I want you to know that I didn't
get into any income tax trouble about it.

Red did not go completely empty-handed for his work
that day, but the story as he tells it in *The Broadcasters*
suggests that NBC was no more generous in the Sarnoff
days than it is in its current General Electric incarnation.
Red knew TV was the future. He did not dismiss it as
many radio broadcasters of the period did. So he asked
NBC for a memento of the historic event. NBC sent a
small, silver cigarette box with an inscription:

> *To Red Barber*
> *Pioneer Television Sports Announcer*
> *in grateful appreciation*
> *National Broadcasting Company*
> *August 26, 1939*

Red wrote that "accompanying the box was a bill for thirty-
five dollars, which I paid. I wanted the box."

Red with Pee Wee Reese, Durocher and Branch Rickey—the Brooklyn broadcaster, captain, manager, and general manager.

Boom Years

RED BARBER WAS TO BROADCAST sports journalism what Edward R. Murrow was to broadcast journalism overall, so it was only fitting that when Murrow returned from Europe after World War II, the first person he hired at CBS was Red Barber, who replaced Ted Husing as the network's director of sports. No doubt Red's journalistic approach to sports appealed to Murrow.

When Hitler was swallowing nations, Murrow's reporters stationed in the various European capitals were linked electronically to share their reports in a "roundup" fashion. As CBS's director of sports, Red did the same with the network's broadcasts of college football games on Saturdays. Instead of sticking with a boring blowout of a game, Red would switch to a reporter covering a more interesting game, in which perhaps the underdog had just tied the score in the second half.

To accomplish the roundup, Red assembled a network of sports reporting talent from across the country. Bill Munday's career was revived by the roundup. Munday was one of the many men in sports broadcasting who became an alcoholic. Red was the only one willing to give Munday a second chance—and it paid off. Here's how Red put it in his book *The Broadcasters*:

> Bill Munday . . . was the broadcaster I have the most respect for. First he was great. Then he threw it away. Next, he fought back. He beat himself. . . . At one time he drank like a fish. But he was a game fish—he swam upstream—right into the Promised Land. That's what Bill Munday always called the end zone—the Promised Land.

The roundup also introduced new talent. Vin Scully, fresh out of Fordham University, went to see Red one day at CBS. There was no work for Scully that day, but some weeks later Red needed someone on short notice to cover a game in Boston. Scully was tracked down and did a fine job. Afterward, Red learned that Scully had had no press box from which to broadcast. He had worked from the roof of Fenway Park and made no mention of the cold, the wind and the rain. Red didn't care for reporters who were overly concerned about their personal comfort. A year later, Red decided to bring Scully onto the Dodger broadcasts, where he remains to this day. And though Vinny is a senior citizen himself now, he was always "young Scully" to his mentor.

CBS sent Red to cover the 1948 Winter Olympics at St. Moritz. In fact, Red was the only radio reporter covering

those Olympics. Imagine Red Barber, son of Dixie, being
sent to Switzerland to cover luge and bobsled and slalom.
Where Red came from, ice dancing was something you did
with your sweetie over lemonade. Red was no fool. He
recruited help.

> RED: I didn't know a thing about it. I had never seen a
> winter sport at all. But Armed Forces Radio had asked
> me to come over early and speak to the troops in
> Germany . . . and Major Ed Link there said, "Gee, I'd
> like to go to St. Moritz and see the Winter Olympics,
> but I don't have any credentials." "Well," I said,
> "you've got 'em now. You come and stay with me and
> keep me briefed." And so it was Major Link who gave
> me the, should we say, the literature, the wordage.
> When I got back, Murrow said, "I didn't know you
> knew so much about the Winter Olympics." I said, "I
> didn't either."

Red was a busy man in those years, remaining on the
Dodger broadcasts while working for CBS, where his duties included doing a nightly program for the network.
Stanley Woodward, editor of the *New York Herald Tribune*,
wrote that Red couldn't possibly do both jobs, and that if
he did, then he, Woodward, would commit hara-kiri in
front of CBS headquarters at 485 Madison Avenue. Red
said, "I used to look for his body, day after day."

But it was Red's body that was in danger. In 1948, he
suffered a bleeding ulcer that nearly killed him. It occurred without warning in July in Pittsburgh, the last stop
on a road trip to "the West" (the West ended in St. Louis
then). In three days he was scheduled to leave for London,
where he was to cover the Summer Olympics for CBS.
After eighteen holes of golf with Connie Desmond and
two other men, Red started hemorrhaging. His description in his own writings is far more graphic than anything
you'll read here, but he lost half the blood in his body in

the locker room of a Pittsburgh country club. At the hospital, Lylah, Desmond and the others broke down when they visited. The doctors talked about him as if he weren't in the room. Red was convinced that everyone had written him off. He decided he was going to die and he concluded that that wouldn't be so bad. He described it in his book *Show Me the Way to Go Home*:

> I was alone. It was very quiet. It was maybe around one o'clock. . . . I knew I was at the brink. I knew I was about to go over it. I knew it, and I didn't care. It was too much to care. I was too weak. Slide on over the edge and down. Over . . . over the edge . . . it was so close . . . so easy . . . and I didn't care. Then there was a presence in the room. It wasn't a person. It wasn't anything I could see or touch or smell or hear or in any manner describe, but I was no longer alone. There was something very real in the room, and it demanded my attention. It was so real, I was flooded with a feeling of complete comfort. . . . I was told . . . that I was not to fear, but close my eyes . . . and sleep. The next morning when I woke I was still in Pittsburgh.

Nowadays, we call that a near-death experience. Sarah Barber says it was her father's first brush with mortality, and he was embarrassed that it happened after a round of golf with some close male friends.

Red was transferred to a hospital in New York. Later, he recalled looking out the window at another hospital, where Babe Ruth was dying of cancer. A crowd on the street below kept vigil for the Babe.

Meanwhile, the Dodgers needed another broadcaster to temporarily help Red's associate, Connie Desmond, cover the games. They contacted the minor league Atlanta Crackers about using their broadcaster, Ernie Harwell. It just so happened the Crackers were in need of a catcher. Atlanta said Brooklyn could have Harwell if the Dodgers sent catcher Cliff Dapper from their organization. So Ernie

Harwell, now in the Hall of Fame, went to the big leagues as the only broadcaster ever traded for a player. When Red recovered, he and Desmond kept Harwell, and they became sports broadcasting's first three-member team. Later, Harwell crossed the river to join Russ Hodges, who was doing Giants games at the Polo Grounds. That's when "young Scully" came aboard as Harwell's replacement.

Red treated himself gingerly during his recovery—perfectly understandable for a man who thought he was going to die. But later he turned this into a sermon on self-pity. He says Branch Rickey, who was running the Dodgers by that time, implied to him that he was malingering and urged him to return to work. Red returned to the Dodgers on September 9 at the Polo Grounds. He had to be talked into broadcasting the World Series and the college football games that fall. It wasn't until Red broadcast a charity football game in Alabama that he snapped out of it. Game sponsors kept taking Red to the wards of the children's hospital that would be helped by the game's receipts. There he realized he was a lot better off than the children who would never walk or function as well as he could.

Larry MacPhail and Branch Rickey were the two most important men in Red Barber's career. They made it possible for Red to *be* Red Barber. They turned him loose and told him to report what he saw on the field no matter how ugly it looked. He was not to be a booster of the team or a shill for the owner. He was to be his own man, and they backed him.

As an example, Red told the story of a pressroom bartender named Hymie Green. Red's broadcast was on in the pressroom, and Red announced that a runner was out. But the ball rolled out of the fielder's glove and the umpire changed his call to safe, so Red did, too. Green remarked, "Listen to that Barber—he don't know 'out' from 'safe.' " MacPhail said, "Let Barber broadcast—you tend bar." Green said, "You can't talk to me like that." MacPhail said,

"I never will again . . . you're fired." The firing was witnessed by a sportswriter who passed the story on to Red.
MacPhail never mentioned it to his broadcaster.

Rickey gave Red the same independence. He told him,
"You're closer to it than any man alive. You do it." Rickey
also told Red that he had a "civic responsibility." This re-
sulted in Red's becoming a spokesman and fund-raiser for
numerous causes.

MacPhail and Rickey were two of the most important
men in baseball history. Red said it was their innovations
that brought baseball into the twentieth century. Many
pages of Red's books were devoted to numerous compar-
isons and contrasts between Rickey and MacPhail:

> Both at different times had attended the University of
> Michigan, both had gotten degrees in law. Rickey was nine
> years older. Neither followed law as a profession. . . .
> MacPhail drank. Rickey never touched a drop in his life.
> MacPhail was often profane. Rickey's strongest expletive
> was "Judas Priest," and he never went to the ballpark on
> Sunday. MacPhail got into fights. Rickey didn't. . . .
> MacPhail was abrupt in his speech. Rickey was a master of
> the language and a nationally known speaker. He was a
> spellbinder.

Red was the perfect man to appreciate his two patrons.
Their contradictory personalities were really the two sides
of Red Barber, the product of the extroverted, storytelling
father and the scholarly, churchgoing mother.

But Red described MacPhail as a Jekyll-and-Hyde figure. When MacPhail had been drinking, he would fly into
rages. He had a nasty habit of firing people, then rehiring
them the next day. Red was on the receiving end of one of
MacPhail's rages and learned his lesson: "Never again did
I stay around him one minute after I saw him take the first
drink—from then on I was already late for an appoint-
ment. Very late."

MacPhail joined the Army after the 1942 season. When

he returned to baseball after World War II, his old job with the Dodgers was held by Branch Rickey. So MacPhail joined with Dan Topping and Del Webb to purchase the New York Yankees. As Red wrote it:

> Here they were—Branch Rickey in Brooklyn at Ebbets Field, Larry MacPhail in the Bronx at Yankee Stadium. They were now in the same town, in the same market, competing for the radio and television audience, for money; both fighting for space in the same newspapers, needing strong promotions, and building ballclubs.

Red wrote a whole book about what happened next. *1947—When All Hell Broke Loose in Baseball* tells the story of a season that began with Leo Durocher's suspension by Commissioner Happy Chandler (in part, the result of MacPhail's conflict with Rickey), featured baseball's official goodbye to Babe Ruth and ended with one of the best World Series ever. The Series enjoyed the biggest radio audience ever, and it was the first one on TV. When it was over, Larry MacPhail announced he was leaving baseball forever. But the 1947 season had a much bigger story than any of these, and Red was no mere witness to this story. He was a major participant.

Robinson

Branch Rickey gave Red a two-year warning. In March of 1945, at Joe's Restaurant in Brooklyn, Rickey told Red that he planned to sign a black player for the Dodgers. At the time he didn't know which player, or when the integration of baseball was going to take place, but he wanted Red to be prepared. Red was *not* prepared. No one but Rickey was prepared; even his own family opposed him.

The strength of Rickey's commitment to integration sprang from a pathetic scene much earlier in Rickey's baseball life. Charley Thomas, a catcher, was the only black player on the Ohio Wesleyan University baseball team that Rickey coached in 1904. The team was checking into the Oliver Hotel in South Bend, Indiana, before a series of games with Notre Dame. The desk clerk would not allow Thomas to register, but grudgingly agreed to let him take the second bed in Rickey's room. After Rickey finished supervising the check-in, he went to his room and found Thomas crying and pulling at his hands. "It's my skin, Mr. Rickey, it's my skin. If I could just pull it off, I'd be like everybody else."

Rickey told this story to Red at their restaurant meeting in 1945. Rickey said he had been hearing Charley Thomas's voice for the past forty-one years crying, "It's my skin, Mr. Rickey." And now he was going to do something about it.

Red knew that if Branch Rickey said he was going to do something, you could bet the bank he was going to do it. So Red went home and told Lylah that he was quitting his job. "You don't have to quit tonight," she replied. "You can do that tomorrow. Let's have a martini." Maybe Lylah Barber had been around Larry MacPhail long enough to know that the world looks different after twenty-four hours of reflection.

Born in Columbus, Mississippi, and reared in Sanford, Florida, where he said he had seen black men tarred and feathered, Red Barber had grown up in a completely segregated world. He said, "In the words of the song in *South Pacific,* I had been 'carefully taught.' " Red would have to make a lot of adjustments in attitude before he could broadcast a game in which a black man was equal to a white man.

RED: I realized that . . . I had had nothing to do with being born white, anything more than a black player had to do with being born black. Therefore, I didn't know that I had something to be so proud about about the color of my skin. It was by accident. And then I began thinking: if I quit, where will I go? I had the best job in sports, all sports, at Ebbets Field, and I had created it. How would I replace it? And we all come down to the bottom line. I think they call it economic determinism. And then I remembered before my first World Series back in 1935, Judge K. M. Landis, addressing the broadcasters . . . said in effect, "You fellows are here to report. You let the ballplayers play. Don't criticize how they play. Just report what they do. And the same thing with the managers. Don't criticize their moves, just report. And the same thing especially with the umpires. Just report what they do. And suppose a ballplayer comes over to my box and spits in my face? Don't feel sorry for the commissioner, just report his reaction if he has one. Gentlemen! Report!

And leave your opinions in your hotel room."

Looking over myself and knowing that the black player was coming—I didn't know who he was but I knew that he was coming—I suddenly heard this voice from the grave saying, "Report!" And I realized I wasn't Mr. Rickey, I wasn't the black player, I wasn't the manager, I wasn't a teammate. What was my assignment in this? Only to report. And suddenly all the scales fell off of my eyes and I had no problem whatsoever. All I did about Jackie Robinson, and the other black players who followed, was simply to report, report them as I did any other ballplayer. And I'm very happy to say that Mr. Rickey was satisfied, and I know that Jackie Robinson was. And I was never criticized.

It's ironic that Red chose to invoke a memory of Landis in connection with his approach to the integration of baseball, for it's probably no coincidence that the event did not occur before the judge's death. Red wrote that each time the commissioner was asked about integration, he would say, "There is nothing in the laws of baseball that prevents a Negro from playing in it." And Red added:

All the men in baseball understood the code. A code is harder to break than an actual law. A law is impersonal. Often a man breaks a law, is clever enough to get away with it, and people think he is a smart fellow. But when you break an unwritten law, a code of conduct, you are damned, castigated, banished from the club, so to speak. You are a renegade, a scoundrel, an ingrate, a pariah.

This is the fate Branch Rickey risked by breaking the code. Actually, he risked more. There were death threats against Rickey and the man he chose to make history. So Jackie Robinson was chosen carefully. Rickey knew that Robinson had stood up for himself and his people as a student-athlete at UCLA and as a soldier during the war.

He was no Uncle Tom. Rickey didn't want a man who would play the fool for white people. That would set the cause back. But so would a man who would react violently to adversity, and there surely would be adversity. Rickey made Robinson promise that he would turn the other cheek, that he would not take the bait and be goaded into a fight over the spikings and the racial epithets that would come his way. Given Robinson's disposition, that must have taken as much courage as it took to face the snipers he was told would be at the games. Long before Robinson took the field, Rickey looked him in the eye and called him every awful name a black person had ever heard. It was a conditioning exercise to prepare the young man for what was to come. He told Robinson what to expect, told him he would have to eat and sleep apart from the rest of the team in St. Louis and Cincinnati. He told him what Rachel Robinson could expect to hear in the grandstands. When the slurs came for real, Robinson remembered his promise, and took some small comfort in the fact that everything was going exactly as Rickey had predicted.

Some of the Dodger players threatened to boycott. When manager Leo Durocher quashed that action, several of the players asked to be traded. A few got their wish. Members of the St. Louis Cardinals threatened a strike, but that action was stopped. According to Red, their leader was Enos Slaughter, who deliberately spiked Robinson on the back of the leg, barely missing the vulnerable Achilles tendon. Robinson survived all this and much more.

The fans took their cues from other Dodger players such as Pee Wee Reese, the Dodger captain and a Southerner. During a game in Cincinnati, Reese put his arm around Robinson; his acceptance of Robinson was a signal to others. And Red Barber was another important sender of signals that year. That most Southern of voices was at what he called "the hottest microphone any announcer had to face." The fans were waiting to hear what Red would say. Red said nothing extraordinary—it was what

Red didn't say that made an impression. He never said the word "black" or "brown" or "Negro" or "colored." He just said "Robinson" in the same way he would say "Stanky," "Reiser" or "Casey." Robinson was just another infielder.

Well, maybe not *just* another infielder. He was the National League Rookie of the Year. And the Dodgers won the pennant. There's nothing like success to smooth over adversity. And maybe the key to successful integration was that Jackie Robinson was putting money into the pockets of his teammates. What were the phrases Red used, "bottom line" and "economic determinism"?

It was more than that for Red because he had looked deep into his soul and found something there he didn't like. Jackie Robinson helped him fix that. Red told me that Robinson had done far more for him than he had ever done for Robinson.

The Barbers paid a price for social enlightenment. It cost them some of their longtime friends. A lawyer and his wife were visiting from Gainesville. After dinner in the Barber home, Red suggested the couple be his guests at Ebbets Field. The lawyer exploded: "No. I'll never set foot in Ebbets Field as long as that nigger is playing there." Lylah said her husband never hesitated. Red calmly said, "We won't miss you." The evening came to a sudden conclusion and the Barbers never saw the couple again.

In 1969, in a book called *Walk in the Spirit,* Red wrote:

> Rickey and Jackie Robinson had made me think. Selma, Alabama, had made me think. So had Birmingham. So had Philadelphia, Mississippi. So had the battle over segregated schools. So had racial riots in city after city. Black Power and Black Muslims and George Wallace of Alabama and Governor Ross Barnett of Mississippi and the riots at the University of Mississippi over one Negro man going to school there made me think.

Red's comments were in connection with an interview he did in Tallahassee after he had retired from big league baseball. He was then a columnist for *The Miami Herald* and had interviewed Jake Gaither, the legendary football coach at Florida A&M, a predominantly black school. Gaither had just signed a new recruit named Rufus Brown, A&M's first white player. The interview moved beyond Rufus Brown to the bigger questions of civil rights. At some point it occurred to Red that he was having his first substantive racial discussion with a black person. Gaither was a moderate and these were the Black Power days. His last words to Red were, "A converted white man—by that I mean a white man who has made up his mind to be fair—is the best friend a black man can have."

Red Barber, who in high school had wanted to join a minstrel show and perform in blackface, was sixty years old and still growing.

Wild Kingdom

THE BARBER FAMILY'S affinity for cats may have predated Red's use of the "catbird seat" expression. There were many cats over the years, and there were reminders of them in the Barber home in Tallahassee. There were photos of cats they had known and loved, Lylah's paintings of cats, ceramic cats sitting in corners, a ceramic cat sleeping on a ceramic pillow, pewter cats in the knickknack case, cat books, cat switchplates, cat candleholders and cat ashtrays. Outside were cat sculptures. My favorite was a cat statue hidden in some tall, ornamental grass near the swimming pool. This cat was crouched low in that poised-to-strike position, as if it were waiting for a sculpted bird or plaster squirrel to pass by. No doubt the Barbers' friends and relatives would see objects with cat themes and conclude that they had just discovered the Barber family's Christmas present for that year.

NPR listeners were apprised of the cat world right from the start. This conversation is from our program on October 16, 1981.

RED: The important business of the week, Bob, which has had my attention, was to drive on down to Titusville Wednesday and pick up an Abyssinian kitten.
BOB: An Abyssinian kitten?
RED: An Abyssinian kitten.

BOB: What are they?

RED: Well, what they are is very, very wonderful. They're ruddy little fellas. I've never had a cat that's so intelligent, so alert, so loving. We had heard about them. Lylah and I have had a total of about fourteen cats. We've had domestic cats. We've had a Persian. We've had four Siamese. We've had a Burmese. And the last cat we had, strictly a long-haired domestic named Bella, and she lived with us, Bob, for over twenty-three years. And when we lost her earlier this summer, it was really like losing a member of the family. And so this little fella, this little Abyssinian whose name is Arwe, he is the replacement. And so far he is replacing beautifully.

BOB: Arwe?

RED: Yes, this is Coptic. We have a professor, John Priest, at the Florida State University Department of Religion. And Lylah asked him to get a genuine, authentic name, an Abyssinian name. Of course, Abyssinia today is called Ethiopia. But in the Coptic language, he got a name for "wild beast," which is A-R-W-E. And it's pronounced "ARE-way." So he is a throughly authentic Abyssinian with an authentic name.

BOB: You wouldn't call a cat Reggie or Yogi or anything like that?

RED: Well, the first cat we had, we called him Sam. And the next one was Archie. Then Salome and then Only Son. And we've had a Siamese called Mr. Walkie-Talkie, and the name for that is, of course, obvious. The Burmese was called Richard the Lionhearted. We had a Siamese called One Too Many. And when I was a patient in New York Ear, Eye and Nose Hospital, the hospital agreed and Lylah brought the cat to see me, and he spent a day and a night with me.

BOB: How come you like cats so much?

RED: Oh, my wife introduced me to cats. My daddy was

a pit bull terrier man in Mississippi. And we've had five dogs—a pit bull, an English bull, a wirehaired, we've had a poodle and we've had a dachshund. But there's just something about cats that speaks to me, Bob.

BOB: The dogs got along with the cats?

RED: Yes, yes. At the time we had the English bull and the dachshund, that's when we got a Siamese kitten. And one night at the dinner table the two dogs went right under my feet and the cat right in back of them. And I said, "Oh, he's one too many." And that's how he got named.

BOB: How 'bout those playoffs, Red?

RED: I'll start thinking about them next week.

We were at it again a year later on November 26, 1982. This time the subject was celebrity cats.

RED: Did you happen to see the Sunday *Times, The New York Times*, for November the fourteenth, Bob? There's a four-column story and a two-column-wide picture of an Abyssinian cat named Tu.

BOB: Not again, Red.

RED: Yeah, but the thing is the headline: "Stolen Cat Leads Police to a Burglary Suspect." . . . This burglar is supposed to have stolen some three million dollars' worth of paintings, jewelry and antiques from a hundred thirty homes around the northern area of San Francisco. And one of the mistakes he made is that he stole somebody's Abyssinian cat named Tu. And that's how the police checked him out and found out about it. And the cat is being held as material evidence. That's a very famous cat. Now, I think that's important.

BOB: Now, you have in the past, of course, instructed our listeners on the merits of the Abyssinian cat, have you not?

RED: Well, we've had one now for over a year. . . . But listen, speaking of famous cats, on the fifth of July 1940, I was doing a ball game in the studios in New York, when we used to re-create them from Western Union. My wife had gone out of town and we had a Siamese cat named Only Son. He was out in Scarsdale in Westchester County by himself. And the Dodgers up in Boston got involved in a twenty-inning ball game. So every so often I'd say, "There goes the five-thirty, I wonder how my old cat's doing." And, "There goes the six-fifteen commuting train, I wonder how the cat's doing." Well, as the game went on, the telephone calls to the station about the cat, you know, people were very concerned. And the next day everybody wanted to know how was the cat when I got home. The *New York Journal American* a couple of days later sent a photographer and a reporter and did a full-page story on him. Later, he was an honored guest at the annual cat show at the St. George Hotel in Brooklyn. So, you know, cats can get into the news. It's not just the fact that they have a sellout show in London and a big sellout show in New York.

BOB: That cat could have had his own show if he'd had an agent and worked on it a bit.

RED: Well, I hope my cat's not listening because the last thing I need from him right now is for him to present an agent.

Listeners were kept informed of Arwe's adventures over the years. By July 13, 1984, Arwe had found an adversary.

RED: Something serious in sporting is going on down here in my front yard. There's a mockingbird that's got a nest and he's got some young ones in there. And you know about our Abyssian cat, Arwe?

BOB: Yes, I certainly do.

RED: His life is now miserable. He likes to go out, but he

doesn't anymore. He's just hanging inside because, I want to tell you, the father mockingbird is a rough customer. He is dive-bombing our cat.

BOB: I don't blame him. Are you keeping him inside or is he inside voluntarily?

RED: Well, for a while. Before the mockingbird, we couldn't keep him in. And now, with the mockingbird, he doesn't want to go out.

And just one week later . . .

RED: Ernest Hemingway said a man's first duty is to defend his house. And I think that's what this mockingbird is doing. Lylah and I are delighted for several reasons, one of which is that Florida has a great many fleas. And now that Arwe is quite content to stay in the house, that means we have less of a flea problem. . . . And also yesterday, Robbit, one of the young mockingbirds, maybe on his first flying expedition, landed in our swimming pool. Fortunately, Lylah saw the bird fluttering there and we were able to fish it out in time. In a few minutes, after it shook the water off, on the way it went.

BOB: Well, I'm glad the cat is okay. After all, it's getting national publicity. There's a lovely picture of you and the beast in the July twenty-third edition of *Sports Illustrated* and a very nice article about you, Red.

RED: I told Arwe about his picture, and he didn't seem to be impressed at all, Bob.

BOB: He seems to be looking the other way. I'll bet he's got his eye on that mockingbird, and I wouldn't blame him.

By February of 1985, Red had a different animal problem. Scott Simon was filling in for me, but Red managed to get a few words in anyway.

SCOTT: Listen, Red, Red. A few Fridays ago, you began to talk about how some mangy squirrels down there in Tallahassee have been filching food from out of your bird feeders. Now as I remember that conversation, I might have been a little short with you. I was sort of thinking, "Come on, Red, this is a sports segment." But I tell you, Red, we have received more letters about your birds and squirrels than anything I've ever seen when you've spoke out about the Super Bowl, or gambling or boxing. So I tell you what—this morning, by popular demand of the American public, let's talk about your squirrels and birds, okay?

RED: Well, first off, Scott, I never said they were mangy because they're very fat and very well fed. And further, my wife thinks they're cute.

SCOTT: Well, I guess she has a point. Forgive me, I was reaching.

RED: . . . I have nine. In fact, I don't have them—they come from these live oak trees all around. And I don't know whose squirrels they are.

SCOTT: Nine! How do you tell the difference between their little faces?

RED: I don't know them as individuals. I just know that they eat up all of the birdseed, and there's no way that I can defeat them. The thing that distresses me is that they drive the birds away.

SCOTT: Well, now, all right, let me read you some of these letters if I can. Barbara Spark of Westwood, Massachusetts, writes to say that she enjoys hearing you each Friday even though she's more interested in birds than she is in sports. Now, she suggests that you buy something called a weighted bird feeder. She says it accommodates birds but not squirrels. And she got hers from the Audubon Society. She says it not only works, but it's also amusing to try and watch your friends the squirrels try and fail to get to the feeder.

RED: Scott, let me tell you, I've had a lot of mail about

this, too, and also from the Audubon Naturalist Society. And I've been sent clippings about all types of feeders. And the only advice I've received that seems to fit my situation is to trap them and take them five miles away, which I am not about to do. But let me say that these are very intelligent and active and athletic squirrels. There is no type of feeder that these squirrels can't get to. Our yard is heavily planted and anything that a squirrel can get on, up to ten or twelve feet—he can jump to it. It's remarkable, their ability to get the feed.

SCOTT: You speak with real respect for their athletic abilities, Red.

RED: Yes, I do. And they work upside down, they climb anything, and they jump on anything. . . .

SCOTT: We got an ingenious suggestion from a gentleman named Phil Weiss of Lauderdale Lakes, Florida. He sent in a drawing which I really can't do justice to over the air for something he calls an anti-squirrel bird feeder. And it uses a homemade funnel made out of a milk jug to allow the birds to feed but not the squirrels. Now, we'll send the drawing on down to you. But you need to appreciate Mr. Weiss's artwork. . . .

Three months later, Red was talking to Scott once again. By then he had learned that Scott had a cat named Lenore. So he gave Scott a reading of Edgar Allan Poe's poem of the same name.

In May of 1985, we had an animal discussion prompted by something that happened on a ballfield:

RED: Did you note that a skunk interrupted a ball game earlier this month out in San Diego?

BOB: No, I didn't see that.

RED: Yeah, that was in *The Sporting News*, a big story, and I wanted to call it to your attention. The skunk just came out of the infield coverings and for eight minutes—not an infielder—moved.

The next month he announced he had put up two hummingbird feeders and hoped he could entice a few birds. A listener from Pittsburgh wanted a progress report the next week. Red said he got his first hummingbird just fifteen minutes after that first announcement, "so I think that one is listening to NPR."

By 1988, someone had sent him Bill Adler's book *Outwitting Squirrels.* He ultimately got a squirrel-proof bird feeder. It's now in New Mexico at the home of his daughter, Sarah.

Red, however, was no Saint Francis of Assisi. His love of animals was not without its limits. Here's August 16, 1991:

RED: Right here, helping me broadcast, is a four-month-old Burmese, sable, male kitten, Arwe the Second.

BOB: Why am I not surprised, Red?

RED: Well, Arwe the First made a serious mistake after he got to be eleven years old. He decided that our television room should be his toilet room. So, of course, he couldn't stay. Now we have Arwe the Second. And as far as I'm concerned, these other feats in the world of sports—they're just wonderful. But when you have a little loving kitten, Bob, it's important.

Some weeks later I asked about Arwe II. He said the cat was forcing him to be neat and to keep doors closed. Arwe was fond of going into the bathroom, grabbing the end of the toilet tissue and racing through the house. An indoor TP job, and it wasn't even Halloween.

A pair of cats have roamed the Edwards household for the past couple of years. I lived in fear that Red would find out about them and never again want to discuss a sporting event. Our Friday visit would have become the weekly cat chat.

Red and I at the only broadcast we did face-to-face, in Tallahassee on October 19, 1990.

Tallahassee

RED AND I GOT TOGETHER on the radio each Friday, but our face-to-face meetings were few. Red and Lylah visited the NPR studio in Washington on just two occasions, and I missed one of them. I guess I was visiting a member station that day for a fund-raiser. Red and I did two fund-raisers together in Tallahassee and another in Gainesville. And once we were on the same bill with Arnold Palmer and others at a sort of Chautauqua program at Rollins College in Winter Park, Florida. That's where I had the dubious "honor" of following Red to the microphone.

We were face-to-face for just one broadcast. "Breakfast with Red and Bob" was a fund-raiser (of course) for WFSU-FM, the NPR member station in Tallahassee on Friday, October 19, 1990, at the Center for Professional Development at Florida State University. More than 120 people paid seventy-five dollars apiece for breakfast, a souvenir coffee mug and a chance to watch the Ol' Redhead in action. Plenty of Red's neighbors showed up, and they were an enthusiastic audience for the four minutes we were "live" to Washington and the rest of the country. Red, who had no hearing in one ear and not a lot in the other, told the group that it was nice to have the opportunity to read my lips. I countered that I was making no political promises (an allusion to George Bush's "read my lips" remark). Red also used the occasion to plug his daughter's book. Sarah was in her final year as a professor at LaGuardia Community College in New York, and had written a book titled *Connections: Using Multi-Cultural, Racial and Ethnic Short Stories to Promote Better Writing*. In addition to doing business, we managed to discuss the World Series. My favorite team, the Cincinnati Reds, was halfway through its sweep of the Oakland Athletics. I pointed out that I have the luxury of being a fan because baseball is not my beat as a journalist. Red never allowed himself to be a fan; baseball was his business.

Almost all of Red's Friday broadcasts for NPR were done from his home, a one-story, yellow-brick rambler in the handsome yet modest Waverly Hills section of Tallahassee. There was a microphone on the desk of his study. Next to the mike was a stopwatch standing upright in a plastic stand. I heard the click of that stopwatch at the beginning and the end of our talks. He used the watch to make sure he had enough time to tell a story. If he was reciting a Psalm or a poem, he would take care to end the recitation at the point when I always wrapped up our chat. Next to the stopwatch was a notepad with "Red Barber" printed in red at the top of each page. The notes he wrote

on this pad always were in red ink, and his periods were
tiny *x*'s. He answered all his mail and had many correspon-
dents, young and old. Sitting at his desk, Red could look
straight ahead through a window. When he talked about
the weather in Tallahassee, he was looking at it.

On the bookshelves were copies of his six books, which
he would inscribe and send to people. There were other
sports books and quite a few religious books. Several egg
timers were on those shelves. Red used a three-minute egg
timer when he did play-by-play broadcasts; when the sand
ran through the egg timer, it was time to give the score of
the game.

Family photos of several generations lined the walls.
There was Lylah's painting of a birthday cake. And framed
in glass was what appeared to be everything one would
need for rolling one's own cigarettes, including a tin of
Prince Albert tobacco. Those items belonged to Red's father, the railroad engineer. More photos were on the walls
of the hallway outside the study. One showed Red standing at a CBS mike with Pee Wee Reese, Leo Durocher and
Branch Rickey. All four men were wearing suits. There
was a first-day issue page of Jackie Robinson postage
stamps.

The CBS photo, the stamps, the microphone and the
stopwatch were the only evidence of what Red Barber had
done for a living. His awards and memorabilia were given
away to friends and relatives. Some went to WFSU in Tallahassee. Much more went to the University of Florida in
Gainesville, where Red's papers and memorabilia are part
of the library's special collections. There's some more at
the university's Weimer Hall, which houses the College of
Journalism and Communication, WRUF (Red's first station) and the Red Barber Newsroom. Enclosed in a glass
case outside the newsroom are several of Red's books, numerous awards, his Bible, one of his egg timers, photos, an
ashtray given to Red by Edward R. Murrow and a clear

plastic paperweight containing a Winston Churchill medallion.

Red won a George Polk Award during his *Morning Edition* years. I got tired of *Morning Edition* and its host always losing the Peabody Award, so I asked our executive producer, Bob Ferrante, to nominate Red. I figured that was as close as we were going to get to a winner. He won, of course. Sports producer Mark Schramm and I posed with the award before we packed it off to Red. It's now in Gainesville near the Red Barber Newsroom.

Red was a member of a dozen or more halls of fame, including the Baseball Hall of Fame in Cooperstown, New York. There was no hint of that in his home, either. He enjoyed the attention, but he didn't seek it. He did not live in the past. What mattered were the health and happiness of his family, the cultivation of his garden, the company of neighbors and friends, the enjoyment of good books and music and the inspiration of the Bible.

The Red Barber that NPR listeners heard was a charmer. He was a wise, witty and well-read fellow who had been around the block a couple of times, unlike his younger partner. The audience felt like eavesdroppers on a friendship. They would listen in every Friday to hear Red and to check on how our relationship was coming along. In the early years, he liked to toss me a question or two just to see how I would handle it. The questions weren't difficult, but they were disarming. After all, I was the one who was supposed to ask the questions, not answer them. I'm sure I know how "young Scully" felt in the early 1950s.

I had one thing going for me: from 1974 through 1979, I was Susan Stamberg's co-host on *All Things Considered*. That's where I learned to be a good straight man. Most of the comic giants were straight men. George Burns didn't get the laughs, Gracie did. Jack Benny didn't have the punch lines—they went to Rochester or Dennis Day. Of course, Burns and Benny knew what lines were coming and reacted to them. I had to ad-lib. Red's humor was silly, but effective. A good humorist can make any material funny. Red's funniest lines were off the cuff. One November day, I wished him a Happy Thanksgiving. He replied, "Robbit, at my age, *every* day is Thanksgiving."

Once, during a talk show, I said the next caller was from Washington, D.C.

> BOB: Washington . . . go ahead Washington. . . . Well, Red, it looks as though we've lost Washington.
> RED: That's right, Colonel Bob, they moved to Minnesota in 1962.

In the summer before he died, Red gave an interview to a garden columnist from Knoxville. He told her to buy small plants and study them as they grow. Then he said, "Of course, now that I'm in my eighties, I get a full, mature plant. If you're young, you can afford to wait. I haven't the time."

We talked once about baseball players still active in their forties. I mentioned Pete Rose and several other names.

> RED: Don't forget Jim Kaat.
> BOB: Right!
> RED: No, Colonel, he's a southpaw.

That's silly, but we laughed.

Red was intrigued by the Iditarod Trail Sled Dog Race from Anchorage to Nome, Alaska. He liked everything about it—the grueling conditions, the teamwork between dogs and their human "musher," the competition and the fact that it was won several times by a woman named Susan Butcher. One year, NPR did a story about the abundance of moose on the course and how this presented a danger to the teams. Red heard the story and we discussed it on Friday morning. I said, "Red, I guess the moose are not a big problem down there in Florida." "No, Bob," he replied, "only the fraternal kind." How's that for teamwork? One of the dumbest straight lines in history setting up a zinger right out of vaudeville.

By this time, I was "the Colonel." He had built up my confidence to the point where I could run with the ball when he tossed it to me. In fact, Red started promoting me. When I was away he would ask my substitute, "What have you done with the Colonel?" The replacement host that day didn't care where I was; all he or she knew was that one had to get up at an unrealistic hour of the morning to sit in for Edwards. Red didn't understand an outfit that didn't know where its anchorman was, and sometimes he'd say so. Then he would say, "I think it's great that the Colonel goes out to raise money for so many public radio stations. It's just a wonderful thing he does." I was never sure whether Red was explaining my absence to an audience that wasn't getting any explanation from my replacement, or whether he believed (as I do) that the insecurity of the broadcasting business is so great that a colleague can never get enough support. Red knew how to take care of those who took care of Red. That's how one survives as long as Red did in such a brutal industry as broadcasting. Besides, he knew good straight men are hard to find.

Brooklyn Dodgers owner Walter O'Malley (wearing hat) with his broadcasters Vin Scully, Red Barber and Connie Desmond at O'Malley's St. Patrick's Day party in 1952.

Farewell to Flatbush

BASEBALL IN NEW YORK would be radically changed by the end of the 1950s, but as the decade began, fans had to be pretty happy. All three New York teams were contenders. In a year or two, the bars and the schoolyards would hear arguments over who had the best centerfielder: Brooklyn with Snider, the Giants with Mays or the Yankees with Mantle? The same argument could involve managers: Brooklyn had Charlie Dressen, the Giants now had Leo Durocher and the Yankees had Casey Stengel. Or the broadcasters: Brooklyn with Barber, the Giants with Russ

Hodges or the Yankees with Mel Allen. All three were Southerners. Hodges was from Kentucky, Allen from Alabama. A fourth Southerner, Ernie Harwell, who had been working with Red at Ebbets Field, was now working with Hodges at the Polo Grounds. Vin Scully took Harwell's place in Brooklyn. Lots of great broadcasting talent was describing lots of great baseball talent.

The 1951 World Series figured to be another Yankees/ Dodgers matchup. The two teams had met in 1941, 1947 and 1949, with the Yankees winning all three Series. Maybe this would be the "next year" that Brooklyn had been anticipating. The Giants brought Willie Mays up from Minneapolis, but the Dodgers made a trade with the Cubs and now had Andy Pafko in left field. The Dodgers had been rough on the Giants: they beat them five games in a row in April, twice on Independence Day and swept them in a three-game series in August. Dressen said of the Giants, "They're through." On August 11, the Boys of Summer were sittin' in the catbird seat. Their lead over Durocher's Giants was thirteen and a half games.

Suddenly, the Brooklyn pitching staff was plagued by injuries and the Dodger bats went dead. Meanwhile, the Giants got hot. From August 12 to 27, they won sixteen straight games. They swept a three-game series from Brooklyn and cut the Dodger lead to five games. In September, the Dodgers played .500 ball, while the Giants won thirty-seven of their last forty-four games. In the season's final game, Brooklyn was not playing for the pennant—it could only hope for a tie. Thanks to a miraculous catch and a homer by Robinson, the Dodgers won in fourteen innings. The Giants and Dodgers had been bitter enemies for decades, and the drama of 1951 was the peak of the rivalry. The two teams split a pair of playoff games. The deciding contest was played on October 3 at the Polo Grounds.

Announcers for the respective teams were told that the

principal broadcaster of each team would get the World
Series assignment. Mel Allen was waiting to see if his partner would be Russ Hodges or Red Barber. Allen was one
of the few big names who was not broadcasting the National League championship game. Barber, Desmond and
Scully were broadcasting it for the Dodgers, and Hodges
for the Giants. Ernie Harwell was doing the game for TV.
Harry Caray also had a microphone that day.

Don Newcombe took a 4–1 Dodger lead into the last of
the ninth. But Alvin Dark singled. Then Don Mueller singled. Monte Irvin fouled out. But Whitey Lockman doubled, scoring Dark. Mueller was hurt sliding into third,
and Clint Hartung ran for him. The tying runs were on
base with the Giants' Bobby Thomson coming to bat.
Dodgers manager Charlie Dressen went to the bullpen for
Ralph Branca. As the pitching change was made, Giants
manager Durocher talked with Thomson, who had hit a
homer off Branca in the first playoff game. According to
Red, who asked Leo about this a few years later, Durocher
asked Thomson what pitch Branca had thrown when
Thomson hit the homer. Thomson said it was a curve. So
Durocher told Thomson, "Well, Bobby, he'll remember
that. Look for the fastball." Branca's first pitch was a fastball, which Thomson took for a strike. Russ Hodges picks
it up from there:

> Bobby hitting at .292. He's had a single and a double and he
> drove in the Giants' first run with a long fly to center.
> Brooklyn leads it 4–2. Hartung down the line at third, not
> taking any chances. Lockman without too big a lead at sec-
> ond—but he'll be running like the wind if Thomson hits
> one. Branca throws. There's a long drive! It's going to be,
> I believe . . . The Giants win the pennant! The Giants win
> the pennant! The Giants win the pennant! Bobby Thomson
> hits into the lower deck of the left-field stands! The Giants
> win the pennant! And they're going crazy! They're going
> crazy! Oh-ho.

In August of 1991, NBC's Bob Costas interviewed Red for his syndicated radio program *Costas Coast to Coast*:

RED: Hodges's call is . . . very interesting. I think he sort of lost his cool as a reporter.

COSTAS: I've heard you be mildly critical of Hodges's call.

RED: I didn't think it was a professional call.

COSTAS: Obviously Hodges was exhilarated.

RED: Hodges became an out-and-out rooter. He stopped being a reporter. He just started hollering, "The Giants win the pennant." I think he said it seven or eight times—"The Giants win the pennant." . . . I don't think that's reporting.

Red's call of that homer was quite different, and the listener does not detect that the speaker was employed by the losing team.

Old number thirteen, Ralph Branca, comes on to relieve now, in the thirteenth meeting of these two clubs at the Polo Grounds this year, eleven in the regular season and this is the second in the playoff set. Branca, who was beaten by the Giants and beaten by the fellow that he comes on to pitch first of all to, here in the last half of the ninth, Bobby Thomson, who hit him for a two-run home run. All right, so it now stands with the Giants roaring back, clawing and scratching. They have two outs remaining. They have runners at second and third, and the big one is Lockman at second base. Hartung, the pinch runner, off third. Branca pitches and Thomson takes a strike. Big Branca called on for his most important job in his baseball career. Well, *everything* is the most important for all of these players as we come around. Here it is. Searing hot. Branca pumps. Delivers. . . . Swung on and belted deep out to left field. It is—a home run! And the New York Giants win the National League pennant and the Polo Grounds goes wild!

Red was silent for the next fifty-nine seconds while the crowd roared. It's amazing to me that Hodges's screams were not picked up by Red's microphone. After the roar of the crowd died down, Red went to a commercial. One of my listeners told me that after the commercial Red tried to put the matter into perspective. He mentioned that a couple hundred Americans had lost their lives in Korea that week. Then he said, "The Dodgers will get over this, and so will their fans."

The Dodgers came back the next season to win the National League pennant, only to fall once again to the Yankees in the 1952 World Series, the last Series to have Red Barber at the microphone.

The story of how Walter O'Malley got control of the Dodgers from Branch Rickey is fascinating, but too long and complicated for a book about Red Barber. Once Rickey was gone, O'Malley made it attractive for Rickey's people to leave. Red was one of Rickey's people. O'Malley was a "bottom line" man; tradition counted for little or nothing.

When O'Malley took over the Dodgers after the 1950 season, he asked Red to choose the man he thought would make a good manager for the club. Red tried to duck the question by saying that wasn't his responsibility. O'Malley was having none of that. Red said he thought the team already had a good manager in Burt Shotton. Nothing doing; O'Malley wanted names. Red finally gave O'Malley a couple of names. O'Malley ridiculed Red's choices and told him the Dodgers were going to name Charlie Dressen as manager the next day. Red just shook his head. O'Malley was another rich guy who amused himself by playing mind games with the hired help.

When the Dodgers had a poor turnout at the gate one day, O'Malley told Red not to announce the paid attendance. Instead, O'Malley wanted Red to have the camera show all the empty seats in Ebbets Field. Red announced the paid attendance and later told O'Malley it was bad psychology to shame the people into going to the ballpark. Ironically, more than a decade later, Red lost his last big league job for *trying* to get a TV picture of a sparse stadium crowd.

In his book *Voices of the Game*, Curt Smith includes a story told by announcer Jim Woods, who broadcast games with Red and with Mel Allen. In 1953, at Toots Shor's restaurant in New York, Woods heard Yankees owner Dan Topping and Dodgers owner Walter O'Malley bad-mouthing their respective broadcasters, Mel Allen and Red Barber. They even proposed a trade, Allen for Barber. The owners of the game's top clubs were discussing a trade of the game's top broadcasters, who were at the peak of their careers. Now *that* would have made a headline. They must have slept it off that night, because nothing came of it.

Red stayed in Brooklyn through the 1953 season as the Dodgers won another pennant and lost yet another World Series to the Yankees. Red had worked thirteen World Series (and five All-Star Games). He loved them. He considered them the top assignments in his profession. Yet he is the only broadcaster who rejected a World Series assignment.

RED: Craig Smith was the advertising manager for Gillette. Gillette in those days had exclusive rights. They didn't share their broadcasts with anyone. So Craig Smith would have his advertising man tell you the day before, "You're on the World Series." And no discussion of how much money you'd get or anything else. And then after the World Series, just days later, he'd send you a little check. And that finally got next to me. I was announced to be on the World Series in 1953, and I said, "Well, I want to negotiate this and have my agent involved." And Smith said, "You get what you got last year. Take it or leave it." So, I left it. And I was not on another World Series. . . . But my father told

me that the one thing that's important is your self-respect. And I felt that I could no longer have it—being taken for granted and kicked around like that.
BOB: As I recall the story, you got two hundred dollars a game for the World Series.
RED: That's right, coast-to-coast television. . . . And I made up my mind and I told Lylah, my wife, when I got that check and I told Bill McCaffrey, my agent, when I got that check, I said, "Look, next year, if the Dodgers win it"—and it looked as though they would, and they did—"and I'm on the World Series, I want to negotiate. I'm not saying how much I want to be paid, but I'm saying I want the privilege of knowing before I go to work what I'm going to get paid." Now, this is behind the scenes, and people don't know that. This is what all those World Series broadcasters SWAL-LOWED from CRAIG SMITH.

On the day that Red was fired from the 1953 World Series broadcast, he and Lylah took Sarah out to dinner for her sixteenth birthday. He told her his gift to her that day was his self-respect.

I've heard a lot of Red Barber over the past twelve years. I've read all six of his books and heard hours of tape. In no other instance did Red hold a grudge about the past. But this battle with Smith and Gillette over the prime assignment of a sports broadcaster's career made Red Barber extremely angry until the day he died. I put three words from the previous transcript in CAPITAL LETTERS to show emphasis. That's how it sounds on tape. He was angry. He even WRITES angrily when he describes the battle in great detail in his books.

It also hurt Red that he got no backing from Walter O'Malley, though it's not likely he expected any. O'Malley wanted Red to shill for the Dodgers. The notion of Red Barber as a *reporter* had no appeal for O'Malley. Red had enjoyed freedom and support from Larry MacPhail and then Branch Rickey, but those days were gone. He called O'Malley to tell him what had happened with Craig Smith. "That's *your* problem," said O'Malley. "I'll nominate Scully to take your place." Red figured that from that point on the Dodgers were *O'Malley's* problem; he left Brooklyn after fifteen years at Ebbets Field. Scully, by the way, did not take the World Series assignment without asking Red's blessing, which he received.

The following is from Red's book *The Broadcasters*, and is included here because it simply is too good not to be included. The CAPITAL LETTERS and the *italics* are Red's, not mine.

The next day I was having lunch at Louis & Armand's when a young dog robber working in the Maxon Agency came over to the table. I don't even remember his name. He got up across the room when he saw me enter and sit down. He swept over to where I sat, so rapidly that he still had his napkin in his hand. In a voice filled with righteous anger, and with sufficient volume for everyone in the room to hear, he shouted as he waved his right index finger at me— "Red . . . HOW could YOU do THIS to . . . *Craig Smith?*" He turned and went back triumphantly to his table. He had done his duty to A. Craig Smith, Maxon Advertising, Madison Avenue, and certainly to God.

Dog robber? Ouch!

Red and Mel Allen with sportswriter Bill Corum at the 1942
World Series in St. Louis.

The Stadium

AFTER O'MALLEY'S BETRAYAL in 1953, George Weiss was
quick to hire Red as a broadcaster for the New York Yankees. Weiss was the kind of boss who didn't bother his
employees as long as they were doing their jobs. If Red
could no longer have the solid backing of MacPhail or
Rickey, then he would settle for the benign neglect of
Weiss.

Red's move to Yankee Stadium was tough on Dodger
fans, but tougher on Red himself. He was starting over
with a new team, a new organization, even a new league.

And he would not be the principal announcer. Mel Allen had been the Voice of the Yankees since the end of World War II. Red had no intention of impinging on Mel's status. Mel likewise respected Red and never treated him as a number two man. They had worked well together on previous occasions during the World Series. For example, there was this handoff during the '49 Series:

MEL: And now, ladies and gentlemen, with a great deal of pleasure, I introduce to you my co-worker on this broadcast of the World Series, a fellow who has established a reputation in sports broadcasting second to none and who has been broadcasting World Series since 1935, so he really knows what it's all about—the Ol' Redhead, Red Barber.

RED: Thank you, Mel. Newcombe makes his first pitch in the last half of the fifth inning, a curveball over for a called strike to Billy Johnson, the stocky, right-hand-hitting third baseman of the Yankees. Very kind words, Mel. And I might say that there have been three fellas pitching so far: Newcombe, Reynolds and you.

This business of being the principal announcer on a broadcast team is more than just ego. The top man on the team dictates how the team will work. In Brooklyn, Red demanded that his colleagues Al Helfer, Connie Desmond, Ernie Harwell and Vin Scully, be fully prepared before the broadcast. Scully tells a story of bringing Red the Dodger line-up card. Red noticed that Jackie Robinson had been moved from fifth to third in the batting order, so he asked Scully why the change had been made. Scully said, "I don't know, Red." This was not an acceptable answer, and it was the last time Scully couldn't explain something. That's how Red trained Scully. He imposed discipline in *his* booth and expected others to obey the rules. Now Red was in *Mel's* booth, and Mel operated differently. Red said that Mel would appear from nowhere at game time; the home team would get ready to take the field and suddenly Mel was at the microphone saying, "Hello everybody, this is Mel Allen." Red said Mel wouldn't even fill out his scorecard in advance. He would pencil in each hitter as he came to bat. It worked for Mel, but it had to be hard for a guy with Red's work habits to adjust to that.

The first thing Red wanted to resolve before starting work with the Yankees was his hearing problem. The hearing in Red's left ear had been deteriorating for several years. A new medical procedure might restore his hearing; it was called a fenestration because it was designed to put a "window" on the ear. Red decided the operation was preferable to being seen on camera with a hearing aid. But the operation was a tragedy. Instead of restoring the hearing in Red's left ear, the fenestration killed the nerve, even though Red's doctors had assured him this could not happen. He would never again hear anything through that ear.

Hearing affects a lot of our behavior. It gives us a sense of balance and direction. It affects our speech and even our sense of judgment, because when it is damaged we begin to doubt what we are hearing or think we're hearing. Watching and hearing Red work in those days, one might have suspected the problem was booze. Red had dizzy spells. People told him he looked "strained" on TV. He told them he *was* strained—he was straining to hear what was being said in the interviews. And he felt sick.

In time, Red regarded his hearing loss as a morale problem. He couldn't fix it, but he needed to get beyond it if he were to function. He decided to come to terms with the word "deaf." This seemed to help. Once he could tell people he was deaf in his left ear, he relaxed. He believed it made him hear better with his right ear. Red also made certain that the person he was interviewing was positioned on his right side. Instead of focusing on what he had lost,

Red concentrated on the hearing that remained. Life went on.

Red no longer was describing the colorful doings in the Rhubarb Patch, better known as Ebbets Field. His broadcasts now were about those smug pin-stripers whom fans of other teams loved to hate. The trade-off was that he got to see Hall of Fame talent playing great baseball. From 1955 through 1964, the Yankees won the pennant every year except one (they were third in 1959 behind the White Sox and Indians). The Yanks had Mickey Mantle, Roger Maris, Yogi Berra, Elston Howard, Bill Skowron, Tony Kubek, Bobby Richardson, Whitey Ford, Bob Turley and Don Larsen. They won with machine-like precision. Many of us thought they were boring. Red didn't seem to mind. Besides, he loved dealing with the Yankee manager, Casey Stengel.

> RED: Stengel was the best manager I was ever around, considering everything—public relations, his ability to judge the players as individuals. And he was an infinitely kind man. . . . I went to spring training camp my first year with the Yankees in '54 after a disastrous ear operation in which I was half deaf. I asked Stengel to tell me about his ball club. And he shooed the writers out of the clubhouse, took thirty minutes, and he told me about the ball club in detail. He was always wonderful.

Red told me that when Stengel held a press conference, he would make a statement, then look at Red and say, "Got that?" If Red's poor hearing had failed to pick it up, Stengel would repeat the statement. And Red thought Casey was extremely bright. Speaking in "Stengelese" was merely a clown act for some of the writers.

Stengel endeared himself to Red even before Red started broadcasting Yankee games. Stengel knew all about

Red's conflict with Gillette, and after the Yankee victory in the 1953 Series, when Red went to the Yankee clubhouse to congratulate Stengel, Casey replied, "Congratulations to *you*. A big league job deserves a big league salary."

The relentlessly victorious Yankees occasionally found a way to make things interesting. Red always said he preferred a well-pitched game to an offensive slugfest. In 1956, he saw a game pitched as well as a game can be pitched. It was Don Larsen's perfect game, the only one in World Series history.

He also witnessed the other extreme. In 1961, on their way to a World Series drubbing of the Reds, the Yanks set new standards for wretched excess in the home run department. Roger Maris and Mickey Mantle sent baseballs flying over every fence in the American League. One or both seemed destined to break Babe Ruth's record of sixty home runs in a season.

The early betting was on Mantle, who had come close before. Years later, Red told NPR listeners how Mantle, a natural right-handed batter, became a switch-hitter: Mickey's right-handed father would pitch to him and make him bat left-handed, then Mickey's left-handed uncle would pitch to him and make him bat right-handed.

But it was Roger Maris who broke Ruth's record by hitting sixty-one home runs. Mantle hit fifty-four. The Yankees were so loaded with talent that each of their three catchers hit more than twenty home runs that year. Bill Skowron hit twenty-eight and must have had a hard time getting attention.

In 1961, Babe Ruth still had a few friends in the baseball establishment who could not stand to see his great record taken from him. These critics (including baseball commissioner Ford Frick, who had been Ruth's ghostwriter) pointed out that Ruth had set the record in 1927, when a season lasted 154 games. Maris's sixty-first had come after the 154th game of the now 162-game schedule. Maris went into the books as the holder of the record for home runs hit in a 162-game season, while the Babe remained the record holder for a 154-game season. It was said that Maris's record carried an asterisk. Major League Baseball didn't lift the cloud over Maris for another thirty years. Red and I discussed it on September 6, 1991.

RED: I remember very well that afternoon in 1961 in Yankee Stadium. I was on the television broadcast and I think I used the fewest words to describe what happened. I saw the ball going into the lower right-field stands and I saw it get caught. And all I said was, "That's sixty-one and five thousand dollars."

BOB: Five thousand dollars being the value of the ball if it was returned, right?

RED: Yes, a restaurant owner out in Los Angeles had announced that he would pay five thousand dollars for the ball if Roger hit number sixty-one. And personally, I never thought the asterisk should have been there, and I'm glad it's removed. Too bad that it's removed after Roger's death and he doesn't know about it.

It's hard to believe that as Mantle and Maris were belting all those home runs, the great Yankee dynasty was disintegrating behind the scenes. And left in the ashes of this great franchise were the play-by-play careers of baseball's two best broadcasters.

The 1926 Sanford (Florida) High School Celery Feds; Red Barber, a senior, is second from the right.

Moments

I DO NOT PRETEND that every bit of conversation with Red was worth preserving. We talked about many transitory subjects, including the games just played or the games coming up. But the patient listener would be rewarded with something that made the listening worthwhile.

BOB: Tommy Lasorda has signed up for another year at Los Angeles. I think of Lasorda and Walter Alston before him. There have been two managers since the time when you were calling the Dodger games.

RED: Yes. After the season of 1953, Charlie Dressen walked into Walter O'Malley's office at Brooklyn with a letter drafted by his wife demanding that he get a multi-year contract. And Walter just said, "No, we just are going to give a one-year contract from now on and that's it. And goodbye." Well, Dressen came back the next day and said, "Well, okay. I'll take one year." And O'Malley said, "You're one day too late. Walter Alston is our new manager." And Alston never got more than a one-year contract, and he was there, I think, some twenty-three years. This, for Lasorda, will be his eighteenth year. And this has been the O'Malley-Dodger policy ever since 1953.

. . .

In March of 1992, owners of National Football League teams decided to end their six-year experiment allowing videotape instant replays to overrule the calls of game officials on the field.

RED: I never did believe in the instant replay because the game is played by human beings, it's officiated by human beings and it is witnessed by human beings. And I think it's just an intrusion of mechanics that takes away something. The officials are doing an excellent job. Sure, once in a while they may miss something, but not often. But I understand that the instant replay people—because you get different angles from different cameras—they make mistakes also.

. . .

BOB: Got a letter from a listener.
RED: Yeah.
BOB: "Dear Mr. Edwards. During your conversation with Red Barber last Friday, you played an excerpt from Red's play-by-play of the catch Gionfriddo made of DiMaggio's long ball. I wonder if Red remembers

what the Bronx Bomber did as he saw the miraculous catch."

RED: DiMaggio was running very happily towards second base. He was sure in his mind that he had a home run. And then he looked and saw as he came into second base that Gionfriddo had caught the ball. And DiMaggio, who always was very impassive in public— one of the rare times, if not the only time that he really showed his disgust—he started kicking dust.

BOB: Shocking.

RED: That's right.

BOB: Absolutely shocking.

RED: And when he got to center field, he kicked a little grass.

BOB: Was he ever ejected from a ball game?

RED: I don't think DiMaggio ever was thrown out of a ball game. I never heard of it.

.   .   .

In February of his senior year, a high school football star signs a "letter-of-intent" committing himself to play for a particular college. Red, who nearly went to Rollins College on a football scholarship, offered some perspective on this annual ritual:

RED: And I thought of two men when I read about all of these football stars being signed. I thought about Branch Rickey and Red Blaik. Mr. Rickey said you can send your scouts around the country and you can gather the fifty finest baseball prospects. Bring them together and you can easily tell who can run the fastest and who can throw the ball the hardest and who can hit the ball the farthest. But he said that the thing you can't tell for a long time . . . is their disposition. And Red Blaik, when he was coaching at West Point, had two tackles. One was a great big boy and the other was a small one. And I asked him why he was playing the smaller one. He said, "The bigger boy does not have depth of soul." So we've got a lot of players signed ... but they're going to have to find out ... whether they have depth of soul. When you're great big in high school, you're running over smaller fellows and, of course, you look good. But when you get to college, you're going to run into fellows your same size.

. . .

RED: I remember a story that Branch Rickey told about a trade he made with Bill Terry when Terry was running the Giants and Rickey was running the Cardinals. And I think this is at the bottom of it. Rickey said when the trade was over, "Now, William, I have your man and you have my man. William, now that I have your man, what's the matter with him?" And Terry said, "You'll find out." And Rickey said, "I did."

. . .

RED: It seems that there are so many unhappy ballplayers today with all this money than there used to be. When I was broadcasting, the players were just delighted to have their jobs. I remember during the Depression, one ballplayer, asked if he was holding out, said, "No, I'm holding on."

. . .

In August of 1991, Bret Saberhagen of the Kansas City Royals threw a no-hitter against the Chicago White Sox.

RED: This causes me to do some thinking, Colonel. This is the seventh no-hitter this year. We had nine last year. That's sixteen in two years. When I was broadcasting—you can look at the records—you could go for two or three years and not have a no-hit game at all. They were very special. For example, when

Vander Meer pitched his two no-hitters, they were the only no-hitters that year in both major leagues. And I'm wondering if something hasn't happened to the batters. Maybe these young ballplayers are not staying in the minor leagues long enough to learn how to hit. Certainly, the pitching isn't that drastically improved.

.   .   .

RED: Good morning, Doctor Bob.

BOB: What happened to Colonel Bob?

RED: You gave the commencement address this week at Grinnell College and they gave you a doctorate.

BOB: They did.

RED: You're now a Doctor of Humane Letters.

BOB: Yes, I think they're the vowels—the humane letters.

RED: Uh-huh.

BOB: Out in Iowa I saw a lot of the crops were washed away. They're late getting started with the season and it looked like rice paddies out there. A lot of places are getting too much rain.

RED: The crape myrtle has started to bloom, and you know what that means?

BOB: No, Red, what does that mean?

RED: That means that, despite the rain, the watermelons are ripe.

BOB: But you haven't seen the peonies of northern Virginia, which are now resplendent.

RED: Yup.

BOB: Yup? That's it? That's all my peonies get? Well, I hope you have a nice Memorial Day weekend anyway.

RED: They told you, Bob, that at Grinnell, that you got all the emoluments that go with being an honorary doctor?

BOB: I don't think they went as far as emoluments. I think rights, privileges and all that.

RED: Well, I've often wondered—I think I've heard of emoluments, rights and privileges. What are they?

BOB: I'm going to look them up as soon as we're through here.

. . .

RED: At eight o'clock on Wednesday evening, did you see the beginning of the public television show on cats?

BOB: I did not.

RED: A wonderful show, a whole hour. Now that's important.

BOB: Well, I'll catch the rerun.

RED: Okay.

. . .

BOB: Some sad news this week. Alice Marble died yesterday at the age of seventy-seven. She won Wimbledon in 1939, and the U.S. National women's singles four times—'36, '38, '39 and '40.

RED: That's right. And in her lifetime, she made the encyclopedia.

BOB: How's that?

RED: Well, I mean, she's in it.

BOB: Oh, really?

RED: There are not too many people that get into *The Columbia Encyclopedia,* I've noticed, while they can still read it.

. . .

BOB: I'm doomed to live in a town with no major league baseball.

RED: Well, of course, you've got a major league team in nearby Baltimore, which is practically almost the same.

BOB: We don't count that, Red.

RED: Well, I'll tell you what. I know you're welcome when you go a lot of places for NPR. But I think maybe you'd better stay out of Baltimore.

.   .   .

In the fall of 1990, the Los Angeles Dodgers agreed to pay Darryl Strawberry more than twenty million dollars to play baseball for five years.

RED: In the game of baseball that I grew up in, that sort of money was just absolutely never envisioned. It's hard for me to figure out. I know that when I was in college, I got dismissed from a class on business economics when the dean was writing on the board about millions of dollars and he looked at me and said, "Do you understand?", and I said, "No, when you get above a hundred dollars, I don't."

BOB: Well, you wouldn't make it here in Washington at all.

RED: No, I don't think so.

.   .   .

Victor Kiam, owner of the Remington company and the New England Patriots football team, ridiculed sportswriter Lisa Olson when she accused some of the Patriots of sexual harassment.

RED: I think this about Victor Kiam. You know he's been doing his own commercials on television. And I would think that right now, as far as women are concerned, if he wants to sell some more of his razors, he'd better get someone else to do his commercials.

.   .   .

RED: Atlanta has gone wild, you know, about getting the Olympic Games.

BOB: What do you think of that?

RED: Well, I think it's just great. And you wouldn't have forecast it right after Sherman went through there.

.   .   .

In November of 1991, Florida State lost an important football game to Miami in Tallahassee.

BOB: Are hearts still heavy in Tallahassee this week?
RED: Well, I'll tell you something. I was around the Ohio State–Notre Dame game in 1935, and the Bobby Thomson home run, and the Mickey Owen dropped third strike and the Chicago Bears' 73–0 win over the Redskins. And I saw the FSU-Miami one-point game, and you know what happened the next morning?
BOB: What?
RED: The sun rose right on time.

With General William Westmoreland in Vietnam in 1967. Red was on a USO tour as a sportscaster and as an Episcopal lay reader.

Desert Storm

RED BARBER NEVER KNEW IT, but he almost became a casualty of the Persian Gulf War. The whole incident never would have happened if NPR management had known more about Red's war record.

When the Japanese attacked Pearl Harbor, Red was almost thirty-four years old. He had a wife and child. He lived in the country's largest metropolitan area. Red was not drafted, but he served.

When the Dodgers played their first home game in April, a volunteer from the Brooklyn chapter of the Red Cross asked Red to appeal to his listeners for blood donations. In one of his books, Red explains that until World War II broadcasters never used the word "blood" on the air, not even in describing a prizefight. It was thought that the listeners' sensitivities were too delicate to deal with hearing anyone speak of blood. Red told the man he would have to clear it with the Dodgers' general manager, Larry MacPhail. MacPhail's response was, "Hell! There's a war going on, isn't there?" Red made the appeal on the air. In the fourth inning, Red took a call from the people at the Brooklyn Red Cross. They were booked to capacity for the next day. This continued throughout the war, and the blood bank in Brooklyn had all the donors it could handle. In time, the Manhattan chapter asked Red to make an appeal for donors. Red said, "It nearly killed them over there among those tall buildings to ask a favor in Brooklyn, but they were driven to do it." Red was enormously proud of his Red Cross work and his USO tours.

In the early 1970s, NPR was too new and too poor to have its own reporter in Vietnam. We took freelance reports from Southeast Asia and devoted our meager resources to covering the agony the war was causing on the homefront. The network had no employee in a foreign country until *Morning Edition* went on the air in 1979. Throughout the 1980s, we had reporters covering conflicts all over the world. But Desert Storm was our first war that involved a major commitment of American troops.

War reporting is an important test of a news organization. The reporters who covered Desert Storm for NPR distinguished themselves and brought great credit to all of us who never left the comfort of our studios. NPR's coverage of the war earned some of the top awards in the industry. They were not won without a little tension in the newsroom.

Our program on Friday, January 18, 1991, was one of the best ever. It was the first *Morning Edition* broadcast following the start of the war. I had lots of live interviews and had to ad-lib my way through most of them because details of the story were changing in mid-interview. With the news wires available on a computer screen in the studio, I could see that the next question I had planned to ask had just been made moot by some development in the fighting. I had to alter the question or change the focus of the interview. This would have terrified me before I started working with Red Barber, but by the time of Desert Storm I had had plenty of experience at hitting the interview equivalent of a curveball (and even the occasional knuckler). Today I am comfortable with programs like that. They're challenging.

I received orders early in the morning that this was to be the first *Morning Edition* with no "returns." The returns are what we call the short, quirky stories at the bottom of each hour. A typical return is the story of the would-be bank robber who writes his hold-up orders on the back of his own deposit slip, which lists his name and address. It's the story a listener is most likely to recall two hours after the program. We call them returns because the program is returning from a local station break at the half-hour. I begin with "Good morning, I'm Bob Edwards." Then I tell the little story, or "kicker," as most broadcasters call it. I end it by saying, "You're listening to NPR's *Morning Edition*." The listener then hears an NPR newscast or whatever the local station wants its listeners to hear.

On January 18, 1991—and on no other day before or since—thirty seconds of music replaced the returns. What was this all about? If we're a group of responsible journalists, why do we suddenly need an "attitude check" just because U.S. troops have been sent into combat? And who were these people to tell me how to behave on the air during a war? At least I had worn the uniform; very few NPR people can say that. NPR's affirmative action program does not include veterans. The NPR veterans' caucus could meet in an edit booth. The returns returned on our next program. I guess judgment returned as well.

The program in question was broadcast on a Friday. That was Red Barber day and there was some discussion of whether Red should be told to take the day off. That's when I got angry. The decision to nix the returns was just silly; a move to cancel Red would be outrageous. Did they think the man who had filled the blood banks of New York was too frivolous to be heard on this day?

Ultimately, it was decided that Red would be heard, though I suspect the decision was made for the wrong reason. Red's spot on *Morning Edition* was the most popular feature of any program on public radio. Member stations learned early that if listeners didn't hear Red at his regular time, the phones would light up. And if a station dared pre-empt Red with a fund-raising pitch, listeners would be so angry that they might not pledge money to the station at all. I think Red Barber was on our program that day because NPR management didn't want to upset the managers of NPR stations who would have had to answer to their listeners for Red's absence.

When Red's turn at bat finally came up that day, he hit a grand slam.

BOB: Well, Red, since we last talked, we've gotten ourselves into a little war here. The debate is going on whether these playoff games for the NFL and the National Hockey League All-Star Game should be played.

RED: Bob, as you know, I was broadcasting actively in World War II when Pearl Harbor hit, et cetera. And two weeks after Pearl Harbor, I was the announcer for the championship game, the Giants and the Bears at Chicago. And as far as baseball went, Judge Landis, then the commissioner, turned to President Roosevelt and said, "What do you want us to do?" And President Roosevelt said, "As long as you don't ask for anything or withhold anything from the war effort, I think it's important both for the morale, not only of the people

at home, but for the armed forces. Go ahead and do
the best you can." So he gave baseball a green light.
And I'm sure that the people in sports today will turn
to the White House. And if the White House wants
them to shut down, fine. But otherwise, I don't know
why. You're not taking anything from the war effort.
And remember, I've done five USO tours. The troops
overseas get very bored. And these troops in Saudi
Arabia, I understand, are very bored. And I think
they'll want to know how these football games are
played, and certainly the Super Bowl. That's my feeling.

Bob: That's right. You went to Vietnam, didn't you?

Red: Yes. I went to Vietnam in 1967 when it was hot,
when General Westmoreland was in control. And I
know that the people were very much interested in
what was going on at home. They keep bringing up
the thing about professional football played two days
after President Kennedy was assassinated. That was
nothing about a war effort. That was just very insen-
sitive. Very poor taste. And Pete Rozelle has said many
times that that's the big mistake he made.

Bob: Of course, there's something else besides the appropriateness of it, there's a security factor, obviously.

Red: How you gonna keep people from getting in a
crowd? Bob, I think the best thing that we can do is
just go ahead and do the best we can with our normal
lives. And, in fact, at the moment, I'm thinking of the
first four verses of the Ninetieth Psalm, which was
written some twenty-five hundred years ago right
where things are hot over there in the Middle East:
"Lord, thou hast been our refuge, from one generation to another. Before the mountains were brought
forth, or ever the earth and the world were made,
thou are God from everlasting, and world without
end. Thou turnest man to destruction; again thou say-
est, Come again, ye children of men. For a thousand

years in thy sight are as yesterday when it is past, and as a watch in the night."

It was a classic. In less than three minutes he had commented on the appropriateness of playing the games and the importance to morale. He had filled us in on the history of the subject while dismissing the JFK analogy. And after remarking on the futility of the security problem, he tied it up neatly with a sermonette. What great TV pundit did a better job that day?

At home with Lylah and Sarah in the late 1940s.

Preacher

RED WAS NOT A FULL-SERVICE COMMENTATOR. There were subjects he didn't want to talk about. He had no taste for public comment on the increasing smarm in sports—the cheating, the drugs, the greed, the poor sportsmanship. He didn't care to say anything about the callousness of owners and executives who had more in common with

Milken and Keating than with MacPhail and Rickey. He
would take a pass on discussion of young ballplayers who
got rich before they got mature, and athletes who squan-
dered their talents and botched their opportunities for
service to mankind.

Some of our listeners may have misunderstood this ret-
icence. It wasn't that he had not witnessed all the above—
and worse—in his long career in sports journalism. And it
wasn't that he didn't have opinions about the ugliness in
sports. Nor was he a "head in the sand" type who thought
it would all disappear if it were ignored. Red knew that
those matters would be discussed by many others and that
adding his opinion to the pile probably wouldn't change
things. He preferred to focus on the positive, the uplifting,
the downright inspirational.

Red Barber was a lay reader in the Episcopal church. He
was authorized by the bishop to preach original sermons.
His sermon topics often were figures in the sports world
who had triumphed over some adversity or who had
shown a dedication to purpose that would be of inspiration
to others. The message was not hammered into an audience, it was gently put before the group, and it was perfectly obvious what conclusion was to be drawn. Examples
included Branch Rickey and Jackie Robinson defying everyone to integrate baseball at great risk to themselves;
Ben Hogan, told after an auto accident that he wouldn't
live, surviving to win three U.S. Opens; Roy Campanella,
cut down at the peak of his career, accepting his paralysis;
Roger Bannister employing science and a grueling training program to become the first to run a mile in under
four minutes, then leaving the track for a medical career.

Those were his favorites, and each is the subject of a
chapter in Red's book *Walk in the Spirit*. The last chapter is
called "The Blessing," and it's about Red's father passing
on a lesson concerning hard work. Without Red's saying it,
the reader comes to the conclusion that none of the book's
subjects achieved success without a lot of hard work, and

that reaching the goal was more satisfying as a result. The book was written decades ago and will not appeal to those who believe that certain rights and entitlements should come our way without being earned—or that bad behavior on our part can be excused because of some flaw in society or because our mommies didn't love us enough. I guess it appeals to me because I've made the same pitch to audiences all across the country at high school assemblies and college commencements. I use more contemporary examples, such as Jim Abbott, who, born without a right hand, has no business in major league baseball. But he's there because he wouldn't let anyone tell him he couldn't be there, especially himself. My former NPR colleague John Hockenberry is a paraplegic who out-reports journalists with functioning legs. He's covered wars, volcano eruptions and other crises all over the world. He doesn't like being told there's something he can't do. Red's father told Red the world was his to conquer; all he had to do was to go out and get it. That's still pretty good advice.

William Barber was not a religious man. He worked seven days a week on the railroad. Sunday was just another workday. Red's mother, the former Selena Martin, was the church-goer. She sent Red and his sister, Effie Virginia, to Presbyterian Sunday school. Red and his mother were very close. He wrote that his mother taught him the difference between quality and trash. She trained him to be quality and want quality. She had high blood pressure and was just fifty-five years old when she died, apparently suffering a great deal in her last five years. Her ordeal made Red angry with God for "betraying" her faith in Him. What kind of God was that? Red wrote, "I did not go to church again for ten years. I wanted nothing from God or His ministers."

Red tells this story in a book called *Show Me the Way to Go Home*. It's my favorite Red Barber book. There's very little baseball in it; the baseball stories are available elsewhere.

But there's plenty of Red Barber in it, and it explains a lot about how we got the Red we came to know on NPR.

There was a religious conversion of sorts, though not the cliché we're used to hearing. He did not "see" God after three martinis, nor did he hear voices from his toaster. Red was not down on his fanny in the gutter with lots of personal problems. On the contrary, Red was drawn to God through thanksgiving.

> My health was good; I kept making more and more money. The broadcasting assignments got bigger, until they couldn't get any bigger. . . . We built a two-story house on two lovely acres in Scarsdale, New York. I don't believe I ever saw a piece of ground with more beautiful trees on it. I had money in the bank. I had a Lincoln automobile.

That's not all they had. Sarah Barber had been born on September 17, 1937, when the Barbers were still living in Cincinnati. They probably regarded Sarah's birth as a miracle. Lylah had had two earlier pregnancies and suffered what Red described as "pernicious nausea" through all three. The first pregnancy had to be terminated. In the second, they lost a son, born three months premature. Sarah's was a difficult birth, but mother and child were healthy.

Once Sarah started Sunday school, Red decided he shouldn't be the only Sunday holdout in the family. Lylah couldn't believe it when Red wanted to join her for services at the Episcopal church. She was shocked again when he announced he was to be confirmed. By this time he had become hooked on *The Book of Common Prayer*—"the beauty and conciseness of the English language, the fact that everything the Episcopal Church stood for was right there between the two covers, and the inclusion of the entire book of Psalms."

Just a year or so later, Red was the chief fund-raiser for

an Episcopalian shelter in New York. That's when Lylah believes Red developed the ulcer that nearly killed him. She said he got it trying to raise money from Episcopalians. Red raised more money from a luncheon with eighteen Jewish men than he raised from Episcopalians. In fact, he told one black-tie gathering of Episcopalians that "Episcopalians know on a conscious level that they can't take it with them. But I have found out that on a deep level of subconsciousness the Episcopalians in this diocese are firmly determined that if ever anybody does take it with them, they are going to be first." He looked over at the bishop, who was nodding in agreement.

During his recovery from the ulcer attack, Red absorbed the Psalms in *The Book of Common Prayer*. They continued to be his chief source of inspiration until the day he died. When he was asked to appear on a CBS program called *Invitation to Learning,* the book he chose to discuss was the Book of Psalms. The Psalms became part of his daily routine. He recited the Morning Prayer before the family breakfast. Before he went to sleep, even for a nap, he recited the ninth verse of the Fourth Psalm: "I will lay me down in peace, and take my rest; for it is thou, Lord, only, that makest me dwell in safety." He recited the last verse of the Nineteenth Psalm before every broadcast: "Let the words of my mouth, and the meditation of my heart, be always acceptable in thy sight, O Lord, my strength and my redeemer."

Devotion to the Psalms continued through his NPR years. We heard that Nineteenth Psalm a time or two. There was part of the Ninetieth Psalm for the Persian Gulf War. Then there was the tragedy of Len Bias, the University of Maryland basketball star. On the day he was drafted by the Boston Celtics, Bias celebrated with too much cocaine and died before he could spend the millions he was about to earn. Red's reaction was to recite part of the Thirty-ninth Psalm.

Lord, let me know mine end, and the number of my days; that I may be certified how long I have to live. Behold, thou hast made my days as it were a span long, and mine age is even as nothing in respect of thee; and verily every man living is altogether vanity. For man walketh in a vain shadow, and disquiet himself in vain; he heapeth up riches, and cannot tell who shall gather them. And now, Lord, what is my hope? truly, my hope is even in thee.

When we did Red's obituary, we ended it with the tape of that recitation.

Among Red's other sources of inspiration was the poem "Invictus" by William Ernest Henley:

> *Out of the night that covers me,*
> *Black as the Pit from pole to pole,*
> *I thank whatever gods may be*
> *For my unconquerable soul.*
>
> *In the fell clutch of circumstance*
> *I have not winced nor cried aloud.*
> *Under the bludgeonings of chance*
> *My head is bloody, but unbowed.*
>
> *Beyond this place of wrath and tears*
> *Looms but the horror of the shade,*
> *And yet the menace of the years*
> *Finds, and shall find me, unafraid.*
>
> *It matters not how strait the gate,*
> *How charged with punishments the scroll,*
> *I am the master of my fate:*
> *I am the captain of my soul.*

Then there was *The Prophet* by Kahlil Gibran. One Friday morning, we broadcast an interview I did with the comedian Flip Wilson. We had heard that Wilson was visiting Washington to help lobby for a Kahlil Gibran monument. I interviewed him about his feelings toward Gibran and why he was lending his name to the cause. Red tuned in *Morning Edition* that day to prepare for his spot with me and heard Flip Wilson talking about *The Prophet*. When it was time for the switch to Tallahassee, Red was waiting for me with his copy of the book. He explained that when he lived in New York he frequently stopped by the Doubleday bookstore to purchase copies of *The Prophet*. He gave them as gifts to couples about to have children. Then he read:

> And a woman who held a babe against her bosom said, Speak to us of Children.
>   And he said:
>   Your children are not your children.
>   They are the sons and daughters of Life's longing for itself.
>   They come through you but not from you,
>   And though they are with you yet they belong not to you.

Now, here I thought talking to a comedian about a Middle Eastern mystic was pretty far out in the first place. Then I'm topping that by talking to a sports broadcasting legend about the comedian's and the philosopher/poet's views on genetics and spiritual nurturing. Is this surreal or what? Flip's work paid off, by the way; you can find that monument across Massachusetts Avenue from the British embassy.

In 1951, Red was drafted as a lay reader by Charles Baldwin, the rector of St. Mary's Church in Scarborough, New York, in Westchester County. Baldwin had only one lung and needed lay readers. But I suspect he also reckoned Red Barber would be a pretty good Sunday draw. Red said he and his wife had misgivings.

> Lylah summed it up at home when she said rather wryly, "Wait 'til those ballplayers hear about you dressing up in those petticoats and getting up there reading the lessons."

That was just what I was thinking, too, and thinking hard. Ballplayers are rough-tongued. That would be all they needed.

The ballplayers heard about it in 1953 when the Dodgers were playing at Pittsburgh and Red was asked to preach at the Church of the Ascension. Branch Rickey attended the service and gave Red a big hug when it was over. At Forbes Field that day, Dodger pitcher Carl Erskine approached Red in the dugout and said the players wanted to apologize for not attending, but they knew that Red understood they had to prepare for a doubleheader. Erskine added that the players were real proud of Red. So much for the teasing that Red had anticipated.

Red got to be quite the pro in the pulpit, if that's not an inappropriate term. He preached in hospitals, shelters and prisons. In addition to the sermon on self-pity, he had one on the Trinity and another on pain. He developed a sermon for the troops when he made USO tours, now in the dual role of sports personality and lay reader. That sermon had to do with facing death in war and facing death as an early Christian martyr. The message was that Christianity was not for wimps.

A trip to Spain in 1953 gave him one of his best sermons. It was titled *"Mira detrás de la capa,"* or "Look Behind the Cape." In the sermon, Red describes a bullfight, and he does not spare one gory detail. He acknowledges his bias toward the bull and says he kept trying to send the bull a message by mental telepathy: "Look behind the cape." Behind that moving cape is the sword. The lesson is that we should know our real enemy. It's not the cape. It's what is behind the cape. I love that one.

On that trip to Spain, Red purchased a *boina*, a Basque-style beret. He wore it to spring training that year. Walter O'Malley hated it. So did Schaefer beer and the BBD&O ad agency, the other folks who paid Red's salary. Their disapproval was enough to convince Red he should continue wearing it. This rhubarb was one more factor that sent him to Yankee Stadium the next season.

Yankee players were no less supportive of his preaching. In fact, their captain, Bobby Richardson, asked Red to organize prayer services in hotel rooms when the team was on the road, since regular church services were impractical for ballplayers who had to report to work hours before an early afternoon game.

Red also led funeral services for four of his friends, including the legendary racing announcer Clem McCarthy. Red felt McCarthy was the best ever at what he did. He said McCarthy's voice "sounded as though he were grinding rocks together at the same time he was talking." McCarthy had been a national figure, and yet there were few people at his funeral. He had been ill for so long that his friends had forgotten he was still alive. When McCarthy finally died, Red was groping for what to say. He recalled McCarthy saying that Seabiscuit was his favorite horse. Seabiscuit didn't care what the weather was like or the track conditions. He didn't care what other horses were in the race. Clem McCarthy would say, "All Seabiscuit ever asked was 'Show me the track.' " Red got a sermon out of that and Saint Paul's suggestion: "Let us run with patience the race that is set before us."

Morning Edition provided Red with another pulpit, the Friday meetin' of the Church of the Ol' Redhead, where we heard ecumenical prayers and non-denominational homilies extolling the traditional values: sacrifice and hard work, modesty in ourselves and charity toward others. These were not sermons preached with the arrogant, self-righteous snobbery of those seeking political office or more time on the talk show circuit. Instead, they were kind, gentle, grandfatherly reminders of what we're supposed to be about. And how could he not feel we had lost our way?

Red recalled the pre-union days when ballplayers were serfs on their owners' plantations. But later he saw the mediocre become millionaires so spiritually bankrupt they sold their autographs to children. Red was close to the game when ballplayers drove beer trucks in the off-season to supplement their incomes. He was glad to be out of it when the prevailing image of a baseball player was a fellow in a two-thousand-dollar suit closing an endorsement deal with his agent over the car phone in the Lamborghini. Charity, in Red's view, was the duty of those who enjoyed good fortune; it did not exist to enhance one's image during a period of negative headlines. But Red made a distinction between those unable to help themselves and those unwilling to help themselves. He had time and money to give the former, but no pity for the latter.

Most people share those values. They endorse the message, if they haven't always been fond of the messenger. Red could pull it off because he had what every successful prophet has had: charisma. His intoxicating allure was something that can be imitated but not copied. It's not something that's traded, sold or inherited, and it can't be taught. It's something that mysteriously remains tethered to its owner and goes with him to eternity.

Red interviewing Fred Astaire about the athleticism of dancing.

Testimonials

RED'S MANY YEARS AT THE TOP gave him plenty of opportunities to meet, and sometimes work with, exceptional people. On March 18, 1983, he said goodbye to two old friends in radio.

RED: This thing we take for granted, radio, that does such a marvelous job here with *Morning Edition*—the landmark of its beginning was just 1920, when KDKA broadcast the election returns of Harding and Cox. And this week I've been thinking that Connie Desmond and I were twelve years old when radio began. And Arthur Godfrey was sixteen. Connie and Godfrey made tremendous contributions to radio. And both of them died this past week. . . . I'm deeply grateful to both of them and deeply indebted to both of them. Connie Desmond joined me at Ebbets Field in broadcasting the Brooklyn Dodgers in 1943. Bob, we worked together in that booth for eleven consecutive years. And he was by far the best associate, the best assistant broadcaster, I was ever around. When you stop to think about it, it's easy to find a good principal announcer. But to find the associate, the assistant, is very difficult because there you have to find the man who has the ability to do the work of the principal and yet is willing to step aside while the principal performs. And yet if the principal announcer is not in the booth, then it is up to the associate to take it and to do the whole thing. . . .

BOB: You worked at the same network with Arthur Godfrey. Is that where you met him?

RED: In the earlier days of radio, Bob, around New York, Cincinnati, where I was, Chicago, you knew everybody because there weren't so many of us. And that's why I've sort of been thinking about Connie and Godfrey and the relative handful of people who contributed so much to, first, radio and then to television. I remember one time that Lylah and I were coming back from Washington on the train and Godfrey was also on the train. In those days he was flying his airplane all the time, but it had snowed and his airplane was grounded. And so we were sitting together talking. And he said, "You know, when I began, I was just a regular, routine studio announcer, talking in the pear-shaped tones. And when I broke my hip, I lay in

Red with bandleader Sammy Kaye on March 4,
1943. They were regulars on a CBS radio program
for Old Gold cigarettes.

the hospital and nobody was talking to *me*. So I made
up my mind, as I stayed in the hospital, that when I
got back on the microphone, I was going to talk to one
person." And I think that's the secret of Godfrey's
amazing, wonderful success. You always felt that he
was a living human being talking to you. And I bor-
rowed that from him. And as I sat at the microphone
in ballparks, sometimes talking on networks, I always
had in mind that I was merely talking to one person,
not millions.

BOB: Godfrey also managed to do that on television,

where I think it's more difficult. He made that transition to television very well, and still you felt he was talking directly to you sitting there in your home.

RED: He was completely himself. And he was very honest. He would not broadcast for a sponsor he didn't believe in.

In April of 1983, Nolan Ryan passed Walter Johnson as the pitcher with the most career strikeouts. Johnson's record stood for fifty-five years. Red told me about two other records he thought would not be broken for a while. Red's old network loyalty was evident in this one.

RED: Wednesday afternoon in St. Louis, at the CBS stockholders' meeting, William S. Paley stepped down as chairman of the board. For the record, Mr. Paley is the most distinguished, creative man that ever happened in the history of broadcasting. In 1928, he began his record when he took a couple of radio stations that were linked together loosely and losing money, and he founded CBS. And you might call him David because he took on Goliath—the Goliath of the National Broadcasting Company, backed by the resources of RCA. And over the years, he defeated them. He founded CBS and made it the number one network. I don't know of any man who has contributed so much to broadcasting and to the history of this country. And that is over fifty-four and a half years. And then Wednesday evening, Bob, . . . on public broadcasting, there was *Medea*, written by Euripides in 431 B.C. That's 2,414 years ago. And Zoe Caldwell as Medea and Dame Judith Anderson as the nurse, as they spoke those marvelous words, they might just as well have been written in the past week. I think those are records that are enduring and records that mean something. Somehow or another, I think these sports records—well, they come and they go. That's my observation.

BOB: I wonder who's out there getting ready to take on Euripides' record.

RED: Well, of course, Shakespeare came along a few years later and did a pretty good job running against Euripides. Both of 'em are still going.

BOB: And Mr. Paley. You can't duplicate those records, because the man was a pioneer. He did things that it's not possible to do today.

RED: You know, Mr. Paley, with his love of broadcasting and his creative genius—he's full of energy and he's got a lot of money, so he wouldn't want anything. Why don't you call him up, Bob, and ask him to come over to public radio and give you a hand here and there?

BOB: Oh, yes, I think I might do that.

RED: You know, that might not be a bad idea. He might be interested.

Red remembered two other important communicators on October 4, 1985. Charles Collingwood was one of Edward R. Murrow's reporters on CBS radio and TV. He was a gifted reporter, an excellent broadcaster and probably the sharpest dresser in journalism. E. B. White was the master American writer, principally for *The New Yorker* magazine.

RED: You and I live and work and survive in a world of words. And our English language is, I think, the greatest treasure we have. I was deeply touched in the early part of the week by the death of E. B. White. His book, along with his former professor, William Strunk, Jr., called *The Elements of Style*, I would think that every writer or would-be writer would buy that little book and study it and keep it. "Strunk" did so much for our language. And another man who did wonderful work with our language, who died yesterday . . . was Charles Collingwood. I had the good fortune to know him. He was an impeccable reporter and an impeccable gentleman.

BOB: E. B. White—who said, if you could have three rules, they would be: simplicity, simplicity, simplicity. Good advice for broadcasters, and Charles Collingwood knew how to do that.

RED: I remember that Edward R. Murrow, . . . who hired Collingwood, one time hired Prescott Robinson. And what he said to Robinson—the only advice he ever gave him—was "Be careful of the adjectives."

Since Red had worked for Larry MacPhail and Branch Rickey, the two great innovative geniuses of baseball, it's a wonder he didn't also work for the third, Bill Veeck. Veeck put the ivy on the outfield wall at Wrigley Field. As owner of the St. Louis Browns, he sent a midget up to bat in one game. Eddie Gaedel wore uniform number 1/8 and drew a base-on-balls. Veeck had success as owner of the Cleveland Indians and later the Chicago White Sox, where he introduced scoreboard fireworks, among other items. Veeck died on January 2, 1986, and I talked with Red the next day.

RED: He was a maverick and the American League club owners hated him, despised him. They wouldn't let him move the Browns. They forced him out of baseball, but he got back. There are several things I remember about Bill Veeck, and I knew him quite well. He was a man of great courage. He lost his right leg in the Marines in the South Pacific, and I don't know how many operations he had, but he never once complained. The last time I was in touch with him was his last operation. I wrote him a note and I said, "Bill, don't single-handedly try to support all the hospitals and all the surgeons in Chicago."

A thing I remember about Veeck is that he was not only a promotional genius and a maverick, but he was a sound baseball man. In 1948, he was the first American League owner to sign a black player, Larry Doby. Later that year, he brought in Satchel Paige. In '47, he signed Doby and then had Paige in '48. And he drew, amazingly, 2,620,627. That was a great record that hadn't been approached before in baseball. Then in that great year, he tied for the pennant with the Red Sox, and won it with a one-game playoff—that's when Boudreau went wild and Bearden pitched with that knuckleball. And then, in a very colorful World Series, he won it in six games. That was the first time the World Series was on anything approaching a real [TV] network. In '47, the Series had been on locally in the East. In '48, they had one in the East and they had another one in the Midwest. They couldn't connect them. And I know—I was the broadcaster. And after that sixth and final game at Boston, all the players had to exit through the third-base dugout, and that's where the cameras were. The Indians were in back of first base and here came Veeck, hobbling along one-legged. I never saw such a picture. All by himself, here is the young, colorful owner of the new world champions. And I begged the TV cameraman to turn and get this picture . . . and . . . I never got [it]. . . . Also, people should remember that Veeck was a man of great compassion as well as moral courage. On that bad leg, he marched at Selma, Alabama.

BOB: He joked about it, too. He said his biggest fear was termites.

RED: Yes, he was a man of great humor. And I repeat, I don't know of anyone who's had more courage unless it's Roy Campanella. I have never known either one ever to complain about the fates.

I think no sports broadcaster knew the history of his business better than Red. He researched it for his book *The*

Broadcasters. So he was ready in March of 1986 when I asked him about an important figure in that history.

> BOB: I want to ask you about an obituary I read this week. Harold Arlin, not the composer Harold Arlen, a different Harold Arlin, A-r-l-i-n, died at the age of ninety. It says here he was the first full-time radio announcer.
>
> RED: The first full-time radio station, Bob, that we have, because we have exact history, was KDKA in Pittsburgh. It's still broadcasting. It was called the first full-time radio station because after broadcasting the election results of Harding over Cox, it then continued with a regular schedule, day after day after day. And at Westinghouse, there was a foreman named Harold Arlin and he was pressed into service. And, of course, he was *the* pioneer. And he would work as a foreman in the daytime, and then he would do broadcasting at night. And then his exact pioneering effort in baseball came on the afternoon of August the fifth in 1921, when he set up his microphone behind home plate, behind the screen, at Forbes Field and broadcast a game with Philadelphia playing at Pittsburgh. So that made history in baseball broadcasting. And then a couple of months later, Tommy Cowan, who was a pioneer broadcaster in New York City, broadcast the first game of the 1921 World Series. But the way he broadcast it was, a newspaper reporter at the ballpark telephoned balls and strikes and hits and runs to Cowan, who was in a studio, and he just repeated what the reporter said. That's how baseball broadcasting began. In the next World Series, 1922, Grantland Rice, the famous newspaper writer, attempted to broadcast. And then the following year, Rice and Graham McNamee broadcast, live, the first network World Series in 1923. Rice told me that after two

games he'd had enough and left it to McNamee. And, of course, McNamee then became an instant star.

BOB: It says here that Harold Arlin did interviews, too. He did sports interviews, show-business interviews, political interviews—he did a little bit of everything.

RED: Bob, it's amazing when you stop to think that most of us are trained to do work, and here's a plant foreman who suddenly walks in to a microphone and starts broadcasting.

Red and I discussed many of his friends and associates in the sports and broadcasting professions. Red also knew a lot of performers from show business. In June of 1987, Red remembered Sammy Kaye and Fred Astaire.

RED: I was sorry to read that my old friend "Swing and Sway" Sammy Kaye died early in the week at seventy-seven of cancer. During World War II, I got a chance to know Sammy very well. On *The Old Gold Hour,* which I announced on CBS, Sammy Kaye was the orchestra, and we had such guests as Georgie Jessel, Lou Holtz, Alec Templeton, Bill Berg, and a young man named Jackie Gleason. Sam was wonderful to be around, and you remember these things. . . . And then following on that program—Woody Herman, Frankie Carle, Alan Jones—I've had a very wonderful life, Bob.

BOB: You've been thinking about Fred Astaire?

RED: Yes. Years ago I used to interview people five days a week on the CBS network. I was there as director of sports. And we had a lot of different people who would come on the air for interviews—Astaire, Ben Hogan, Joe Louis, Cardinal Spellman one time, ex-President Herbert Hoover and, of course, ballplayers like Musial, Kiner, DiMaggio. I was interested in interviewing Astaire to find out the correlation between his dancing and athletic ability. And to my surprise he said, "Well, I wouldn't say that dancing comes so easily to me. I work at it. I practice hour after hour." And suddenly you see a man who does something so effortlessly—seemingly effortlessly—and you find out that each of us who are genuine professionals pays a price.

Yankees general manager Ralph Houk (second from right) with announcers Jerry Coleman, Joe Garagiola and Red Barber in 1964, just after the firing of Mel Allen.

Yanked

RED WAS CONTENT as a Yankees announcer as long as George Weiss was running the front office. Weiss and the field manager, Casey Stengel, believed in spending the money to buy the young prospects who kept the Yankees winning. Red blamed owners Del Webb and Dan Topping for the demise of the Yankees. He said it began when they started "nursing their money." First, they gave Weiss a low ceiling on spending. Then Stengel and Weiss were given the boot—not because they were losing, but because they cost too much money. The playing field was sold to the

Knights of Columbus. The great stadium on that field was sold to a man who gave it to his alma mater, Rice University. Webb and Topping had nothing left but the franchise name and the players. Then, in 1964, they sold them—to CBS.

Topping once had been the owner of the Brooklyn Dodgers football franchise and had a serious contract dispute with Red over the broadcasts of the games. Red told an interviewer, "Dan Topping inherited his money. He never earned a nickel. And I have learned to beware any man born rich because they don't understand fellas that earn a living."

Red had a number of health problems during his Yankee years. There was the tragic operation that severed the nerve in his ear. His stomach problems continued, and he lost two-thirds of his stomach in a 1960 operation. He had a heart attack in 1964 and phlebitis that same year. Red said at this point he would have understood if Dan Topping had told him he should retire. But the Yankees kept him on, and Red felt great after 1964. He said he didn't even have a cold.

Red did not endear himself to CBS or to the sponsor, Ballantine beer. He didn't like the way they packaged the pre-game and post-game shows that were his on-the-air responsibility. He said that Ballantine was not presenting the programs with any sense of style or class and that the New York fans identified more with the new expansion Mets as a result. He said that CBS was wasting millions promoting "lousy television shows" and not putting any money into improving the Yankees. Red's candor may have been appreciated by MacPhail and Rickey, and even Weiss, but his new employers were not used to hearing this from the hired hands.

The impending disintegration of the Yankees dynasty showed up first in the broadcast booth. When Red joined the Yankees, he became part of a three-man team of professional broadcasters. But one by one they were replaced by jocks—former athletes with no professional broadcast training. The first to go was Jim Woods. Ballantine beer wanted a spot in the booth for Phil Rizzuto, the ex–Yankee shortstop, so Woods was fired. Red wrote that Woods was "the best associate broadcaster in the trade," an opinion shared by Curt Smith, who wrote the definitive book on baseball broadcasters, *Voices of the Game*. Woods worked with Mel Allen, Red Barber, Russ Hodges and Bob Prince, among others—not bad company.

Ballantine also wanted another ex–Yankee infielder selling its beer and broadcasting Yankee games. The company asked Red to take a one-third cut in pay in an already negotiated contract to make room on the payroll for Jerry Coleman. Red refused. The next year, Ballantine hired Coleman anyway. That made four men in the booth, two broadcasting legends and two jocks.

Mel Allen was fired at the end of the 1964 season. It's nearly thirty years later and I *still* can't think of the Yankees without hearing Mel's voice. The Yankees wouldn't even let their principal broadcaster have one more World Series. Red said the job was Mel's life—the wife and children he never had. Here's how Red tells the story in *The Broadcasters:*

> When I got to the booth about fifteen minutes before air time, Mel was already there. He was sitting in his place. He was staring across the ball field. He didn't speak. I don't think he knew where he was. He was numb. . . . He was the saddest-looking man I have ever seen. He was in a nightmare. He was desolate, stricken. And he didn't know I knew. We had six games to do together in three nights. . . . When air time came, I touched him on the shoulder, shook him slightly. He looked at me, blinked, turned to the mike, and said, "Hello everybody . . . this is Mel Allen." How he did his work, I don't know. Doing mine was hard enough. . . . Word had gotten out that Rizzuto would be on the series. Bob Fishel [the Yankees' public relations man] told me he dreaded each day because Mel was on the phone

with either Topping or him—all the time. Mel could not believe he wouldn't be on the series, could not accept he wasn't the Voice of the Yankees, until he wasn't.

When Mel was fired, Red asked to be promoted to principal broadcaster with the authority to order Rizzuto to go into the dugouts and do preparation. He also wanted some say in the hiring of the new man. His intention was to bring in another young broadcaster and train him, as he did with Vin Scully in Brooklyn. The Yankees agreed, and they gave him a raise to fifty thousand dollars.

The St. Louis Cardinals beat the Yankees in the World Series, the last the Yanks would play for a dozen years. The next day, the Yankees fired manager Yogi Berra. A few days later, Red was told that Perry Smith of NBC had been hired as vice-president for radio and TV for the Yankees. It was Smith who would have the authority to hire, fire and assign announcers. The promises made to Red a few days earlier meant nothing. Weeks later, Smith and the Yankees threw a party to introduce their new announcer, Joe Garagiola.

In later years, Red Barber and Joe Garagiola said nice things about one another, but Red did not always speak well of the former Cardinal catcher. He had watched Garagiola broadcast the 1964 World Series and hated his work. The rules of sports broadcasting are pretty simple: the play-by-play announcer describes the action, then the color analyst makes an observation if it's appropriate. Red felt that if Garagiola had ever heard this procedure explained, he paid it no mind. Joe loved the microphone, and he loved it even when it wasn't his. He worked as if he were paid by the word. If he was doing color, he'd interrupt the play-by-play announcer in mid-sentence. Red believed this was highly unprofessional. And now he was being told this man was to be his colleague. Red would be the only professional broadcaster working with two infielders and a catcher.

Sensing the shift in the winds, Red sought reassurance from his old buddy Larry MacPhail, whose son, Bill, had followed Red as director of sports for CBS. Through the back channels, Red was told that everything was all right. He had nothing to fear.

In 1966, CBS purchased Dan Topping's last ten percent of the New York Yankees. Topping was out; Mike Burke was in. And while someone at CBS had warned him to watch his back around Burke, Red started rationalizing. He had come to believe that Topping was not a great patron of his. Burke was a CBS man, and CBS was the Cadillac of broadcasting. It respected broadcasters. Red had been director of sports at CBS for nine years and CBS founder William Paley had given Red his hiring interview. Venerable CBS president Frank Stanton had thanked Red personally for thinking of the company first in stepping aside when CBS decided it needed a full-time sports director. Maybe this could be for the best. But, as Red wrote, "It is a very foolish thing to allow yourself to think what you want to think. It can be very costly."

The 1966 season was a Yankee fan's worst nightmare. The Yankees were tenth in a ten-team league. Just two years earlier, they had completed a ten-year dynasty. They had owned the game. Now they were done. Being the voice of a loser was not a new situation to Red; he had broadcast the games of teams in similar situations in Cincinnati and Brooklyn. The reporter in him almost enjoyed this kind of story. When a team is on the bottom, it has nowhere to go but up. Rebuilding can be exciting when you're watching the pieces come together. Of course, that's a reporter's perspective; it's not the view of the subject of those reports—particularly when the subject is paying your salary.

With two weeks remaining in that miserable season, the Yankees were to play the White Sox at Yankee Stadium. It rained and there was fog. The game was called off. It was called off again the next day. Red saw a story in *The New*

York Times about the Cubs playing before the smallest crowd of the season at Wrigley Field. It also was the smallest crowd that season in the National League. To reporter Red Barber, here was a story.

More fog and rain dampened the third day, but the game was played. Yankee Stadium then had 82,000 seats. On September 23, 1966, just 413 were occupied. It was obvious to Red: attendance of 413 in "The House That Ruth Built"—that was the story. It was a dark day in the history of the Yankees, and no amount of public relations could get around that. He knew that the newspapers would be on top of the story, and they were. In the next day's New York *Daily News*, there was a photo of Mike Burke sitting by himself in the stands on his first day as the Yankees' president. That was much more interesting than the sorry play on the field in a meaningless game.

Broadcasting the game on TV, Red asked his director for a camera shot of the crowd. This was television, a picture medium, and the most important picture was the empty stadium. He wanted the camera operator to pan the empty seats, and he wanted a shot of Mike Burke sitting alone. He wanted to say that Burke couldn't ask for a better day to take the job; when the club's fortunes improved, as they surely would, Burke could remind everyone what things were like when he took over.

Red did not get the shot, though he asked again and again. In fact, the crew was "telescoping" the whole broadcast to keep the cameras off the stands. They would not follow line drives into foul territory. The picture was cropped so viewers saw only the infield and outfield. Red later learned that Perry Smith himself was in the control room, though Red suspected that Smith was getting his orders from Burke. But Red wasn't going to ignore the story, even if he couldn't get the cameras to illustrate it. He didn't want the newspapers to say that Red Barber had ignored the obvious. So he told the viewers, "I don't know what the paid attendance is today—but whatever it is, it is

the smallest crowd in the history of Yankee Stadium . . .
and this smallest crowd is the story, not the ball game."
That was a Thursday. The Yankees played the Red Sox on
Friday, Saturday and Sunday. Those were the last big
league games on which Red Barber did play-by-play.

Monday was an off-day. On Tuesday, the team would
leave New York for Washington and its final road games
against the Senators. Red decided he should meet with
Mike Burke on Monday to make plans for the 1967 season. The Barbers had moved to Florida, and Red was staying in a New York hotel suite while finishing out the
season. The suite had a kitchenette overlooking Central
Park, and Red invited Burke to join him there for breakfast. Red planned to make English muffins. He selected a
melon and some fine Colombian coffee. On Sunday night,
Red got a call from Perry Smith saying Red should meet
Burke at the Plaza Hotel instead. That was interesting.
How did Smith know about Red's scheduled meeting with
Burke?

On Monday morning, Red started for the Plaza. He took
with him a book titled *Best Sports Stories 1966*, for which he
had been a judge. He had heard Burke speak of a son and
he intended the book as a gift for the boy. Breakfast began
and ended with a single cup of coffee. Red presented the
book and remarked that it was amazing that such good
writing could be accomplished in the noise and confusion
of the press box. Burke broke through the chitchat.
"There is no reason for us to be talking this way," he said.
"We have decided not to renew your contract." That was
it. Thirty-three years of play-by-play were over.

It was a good run. Somehow he had managed to thrive
for more than three decades in a world ruled by broadcasting executives, advertising agencies, corporate lawyers
and sports moguls. And he did it while being his own
independent self. But the day had come when being baseball's best broadcaster was not enough.

Red made the next move. It was a pre-emptive strike.

He telephoned the papers to say his piece before the Yankees could call a press conference and put their own spin on the matter.

At the firing breakfast, Burke had added insult to injury. He cautioned Red against doing anything unprofessional in his final Yankee broadcasts. I can just imagine how Red wanted to reply to Burke. Red insisted on doing the final three games and pointed out that he had a contract for those games. He planned a graceful exit. But Burke needn't have worried. All the Washington games were rained out. The Ol' Redhead never got to say good-bye.

Ted Williams in his prime gave Red one interview each year—
but *only* one.

Florida

HE COULD HAVE CONTINUED. When the first warning signs
appeared with the Yankees, he thought of switching to the
Atlanta Braves. If he had, he might still have been at the
microphone when Hank Aaron made history as the game's
most productive home run hitter. That would have been a
fitting way to go out—he had called the game when Roger
Maris broke Babe Ruth's single-season record. St. Louis
was another possibility; when Jack Buck took over from
Harry Caray on the Cardinal broadcasts, he asked Red to
become his partner. Red thanked Buck and politely de-

clined. When that telephone call was over, Lylah Barber, who had been listening from across the room, said Red would have needed a new wife if he had said yes to Buck. She liked having her husband home.

Lylah was probably a major factor in Red's decision to remain out of the game. Their daughter, Sarah, was a grown woman by this time. She was teaching elementary school at 127th Street in Harlem and would eventually become an English professor at LaGuardia Community College. Lylah had set up house at Key Biscayne and missed Red when he was traveling with the Yankees. Red said many times that while Mike Burke certainly didn't mean to do him any favors, he had given Red a new life. After a few weeks of bitterness over getting fired, Red concluded he had had enough of being a "broadcasting hobo." Florida had nurtured the Barbers as children, and now they were going home. Red felt guilty about Lylah, whose nursing career ended when she married Red. During those New York years, she had trouble adjusting to the role of suburban housewife, and she was very lonely. Red often asked me about my wife, Sharon, and how she was doing. Then he would remark on the great sacrifices made by the spouses of broadcasters because their mates travel often and work at odd hours, even on weekends and holidays. This had the effect of reinforcing my guilt over a family that puts up with my strange sleeping schedule and frequent road trips.

Red was just fifty-eight years old when he left the treadmill of daily broadcasting, but he had had some serious health problems, and he certainly couldn't have figured he would get another twenty-six years. So he made them count. He was one of the most unretired pensioners I ever met. He did some TV work in Miami. He wrote a column for *The Miami Herald*. Later, he wrote for the *Tallahassee Democrat* and *The Christian Science Monitor*. He reviewed books. He did voice-over narrations for films and videos. He did some work with Turner Broadcasting. He wrote for magazines. He did speaking engagements and continued his church work. He wrote five books, giving him six altogether. He did more than six hundred broadcasts for NPR. This is retirement?

In New York, the Barbers had been celebrities. In her book *Lylah,* Red's wife recalls a party thrown by *New York Post* columnist Leonard Lyons in honor of the actress Ethel Barrymore on her seventieth birthday. Lyons asked Barrymore whom she wanted for guests, and she named only two people: Joe DiMaggio and Red Barber. It turned out to be some party! Leonard Bernstein and Frank Loesser entertained on piano. Abe Burrows did original comedy skits. Eddie Albert dropped in after his show had played for the evening. So did Ezio Pinza, who was then starring in *South Pacific.* Herbert Bayard Swope was there, and Lylah knew the journalist had been a onetime beau of the guest of honor. Barrymore kept Joltin' Joe and the Ol' Redhead on either side of her. Lylah said she didn't do badly either—she was seated between John Steinbeck and William Saroyan, who traded literary observations throughout the evening.

The Barbers had season tickets to the Met and often enjoyed the theater. Mary Martin entertained Lylah and Sarah backstage. After his opening night in *The Rope Dancers,* Art Carney and his wife, Jean, had drinks with Red and Lylah at Sardi's and enjoyed reading the first reviews.

Branch Rickey had the Dodgers train in Havana when Jackie Robinson first joined the team because the Florida towns would not have welcomed an integrated club. While in Cuba, the Barbers dropped in at the Floridita bar and were joined at their table by Ernest Hemingway and his fourth wife, Mary Welsh.

All of that was behind them now in retirement. If the Barbers missed rubbing elbows with the rich and famous, they didn't complain. Besides, now there was time to do all of the things they had wanted to do. In 1980, Red sent some old interview tapes to NPR sports producer Ketzel Levine. He enclosed this note:

> I had sworn that the first summer I was out of baseball I'd buy a new car and drive to and around the Rocky Mountains. 1967 was it. I bought a Lincoln and started west with 400 miles on the car. I was doing a Sunday column for *The Miami Herald,* so I did interviews here-and-there for column material to be mailed back. By chance, the Cubs were playing the White Sox their annual exhibition at the White Sox' park. I got interviews with both [Eddie] Stanky, then White Sox manager, and [Leo] Durocher, then Cub manager—and left the park, picked up the girl I was traveling with, went to the Pump Room and had a lovely dinner. I didn't stop to worry about how the poor folks were doing.

The Barbers saw a lot of America on this trip. They drove through the Badlands, the Rockies, the Tetons, Sun Valley and Craters of the Moon. They visited the Mormon Tabernacle in Salt Lake City and went nightclubbing in Las Vegas, then took the southern route home—the *deep* southern route, through Mexico.

Home was now a house Lylah called "pure developer" on Mashta Island. But it had beautiful views of Biscayne Bay and Smuggler's Cove. She hired an architect to "finesse it into a little Japanese farmhouse." She was happy with the results and said it was a great place to watch sunsets.

Boom times arrived for Key Biscayne, and Mashta Island was no longer the quiet little place the Barbers had enjoyed. Rich retirees were building year-round homes and the developers were busy. The view of Smuggler's Cove disappeared and the view of Biscayne Bay was about to go when the Barbers decided it was time to move on.

The choice this time was Tallahassee, where Lylah had been so happy during her college years. That college was Florida State College for Women, where Lylah Scarbor-

ough was one of the three candidates for the school's first
B.S. degrees in nursing. Now it was Florida State University, a co-educational school with an enrollment of twenty-
five thousand students and one of the top football
programs in the country. Tallahassee was no longer the
Southern backwater it was in Lylah's college days.

In her book, Lylah said old friends and new welcomed
the Barbers in Tallahassee style with armloads of azalea
and camellia blossoms. The new neighbors got right into
the spirit and planted the garden Red described so often
to NPR listeners. There were twenty-five pine trees in the
backyard. Five of them were uprooted to make room for a
small, oval pool. Gene Ellis of Tallahassee Nurseries
brought in two large southern magnolia trees. There were
ligustrum and redtop hedges, a banana shrub, azaleas, camellias and five cypress trees. Sculptures included what
Lylah described as "an English lead figure of a young girl
holding a bird in her hand." Nature did the rest. Nearing
the end of her book, Lylah wrote that "a mockingbird
outside my window is selling a bill of goods to his lady
love." Maybe it was the same mockingbird that would
someday dive-bomb the Barbers' cat.

A New Audience

"I DON'T LIKE SPORTS, but I love Red Barber." If public radio stations had collected a dollar for each time they heard that phrase, they could have skipped a fund-raiser, maybe two.

When Red joined *Morning Edition,* he renewed a radio relationship with some old fans. Some other listeners were transplanted Brooklynites who could recall hearing that familiar voice coming through the shop and apartment windows and filling the streets of Flatbush. But for most of our listeners, Red was neither a sports figure nor a nostalgia act. These particular listeners were hearing Red Barber for the first time. After one or two of Red's broadcasts, listeners caught on to the fact that Red's chats had as much to do with sports as the wonderful foolishness on *Car Talk* has to do with cars.

The broadcasting business doesn't say that someone has personality. Broadcasting says someone *is* a personality, and someone so defined is one of broadcasting's stars. At one time, the category included Arthur Godfrey, Fred Allen and Stan Freberg. Today, with few exceptions, the stars of radio are the foul-mouthed disc jockeys and talk show hosts who feel they need to shock their listeners to get attention. The listener who stays with such a "personality" does so not because he expects to hear something interesting and enlightening, but rather to hear what his fellow juvenile is going to get away with next. Not the basis for a healthy relationship. I can understand if some of the more balanced minds in society gave up on radio. But to hear Red Barber on NPR was to be reminded of what the fuss was all about years ago. Here was someone you wanted to hear more often, someone you would have over to your house if you could, someone you would like to introduce to your friends and family.

Red Barber *was* family to some listeners in the sense that the audience embraces those of us who work in public broadcasting. And for many listeners, Red was a reminder of a father, a grandfather or a favorite uncle they had—or wished they had.

John Stanley of New York wrote often to *Morning Edition*. He was such a gifted writer that his letters were more like memoirs. NPR's Sean Collins, with help from actor Richard Bauer, turned them into beautiful pieces of radio. The first was inspired by Red Barber. Stanley recalled his grandfather "seated in his Morris chair in his den. The three windows and the bay window open and the sound of baseball coming through the grand Atwater-Kent radio. And the Depression pushed away, and the sounds of Hitler and Munich and all the rest suspended for the afternoon."

Red had a somewhat different effect on those of us at NPR who worked with him. We loved him too, but we also got to know what we called the "flinty" side of his personality.

The *Morning Edition* sports producer was NPR's contact with Red Barber. The first one, Ketzel Levine, left the staff and became a freelance reporter in London, doing news, features and some sports for NPR programs. Eventually, she left broadcasting and now runs a nursery—so she should know her camellias. Her successor was John Ogulnik, now one of NPR's live events producers. The incumbents are Mark Schramm and Tom Goldman. It was

Schramm who had the most contact with Red in those last few years, and he was the producer of the two call-in shows I did with Red.

The sports producer called Red each Thursday at precisely 10:00 A.M., not 9:59 and not 10:01. Ogulnik recalls making the call at 10:20 or so and getting a lecture from Red about responsibility. Red said something about how he and Lylah had made some plans for the morning and now those plans were jeopardized by the lateness of the hour. This is exactly the type of thing Red did with Scully, Desmond and anybody else who ever worked with him. Some of them didn't care for that kind of treatment; they were the types who tried to breeze through their careers with no heavy lifting, believing that discipline was something for the Army, not for the broadcasting of a game. But Scully profited from Red's lessons, and he's in the Hall of Fame today. John Ogulnik is not going to the Hall of Fame without a ticket, but he profited, too. Today he's in a job that requires him to take care of a hundred little details to ensure a successful program. I'm betting that John still hears lectures about preparation in that Mississippi voice, telling him the call is to be placed at 10:00 A.M., eastern time.

Schramm was born a detail man and Red reinforced this tendency. In May of 1992, Red wanted to know how many musicians play in the New York Philharmonic. Schramm made some calls and learned that the answer was 106. The next day, Red told me about his daylilies, followed by this:

RED: And Tuesday night, I thought it was just wonderful on public television to see and hear the New York Philharmonic under Kurt Masur, and especially when they did the Tchaikovsky Fifth. It restored my feeling about mankind, because here and there man can function together. You had 106 musicians and the music was just wonderful.

A seemingly minor detail was important to Red. Schramm says that having worked with Red, he now can work with anyone.

The Thursday call to Red had two purposes. First, we wanted to know if he felt up to doing the broadcast. The other reason was to determine what he might want to talk about the next day. Though Red always said he would discuss "whatever the Colonel wants to talk about," he seldom did. Instead, the subject was his to choose, and we hoped to pick up a hint by calling him on Thursday. After the usual opening pleasantries, Red would ask Mark Schramm how the Colonel was doing. So Mark would tell him some piece of personal information about my family or me that I would never share with a national radio audience. Some *Morning Edition* listeners know my children's birthdays because of Red Barber. Next, Mark would relay to Red my brilliant idea for some fascinating discussion of a truly significant development in the world of sports. But Red would tell Mark, "No, young fella, I don't think anyone's really interested in that." Then Mark would go to item two on my list and Red would tell him, "I think people have heard enough about that." Item three would be a swinging third strike, so Mark would say, "Well, what do *you* want to talk about, Red?" At this point, Red might volunteer that some personal or professional anniversary was occurring that week. That was always welcome to hear. But, more often than not, he would want to talk about the many sports books he had received in the mail that week. He *always* received many sports books in the mail because publishers quickly learned that Red would mention each and every one of them. Librarians loved him; the mail carrier probably took a different view. I was glad to talk books with Red if I felt he had a genuine perspective to offer. I didn't want him plugging books, I wanted him addressing the subjects of the books through his own experience.

Lacking an anniversary, a book on which he had a unique perspective or a current sports story on which he cared to comment, we would "wing it." I can't count the number of times this happened, but I know it occurred more often than I care to remember. I regarded it as the ultimate radio test, an unrehearsed discussion of no particular subject with a fellow who has no patience for someone who isn't properly prepared. There's at least one contradiction in there somewhere. But it worked. It sounded fine on the air because listeners just wanted to hear Red. It didn't matter if we weren't talking about the headline story in that morning's sports section. Frankly, I preferred a chat that had a beginning, a middle and an end. I guess it's just a storyteller's bias of mine. We had more than a few that followed that formula.

Red was unpredictable. If he sounded enthusiastic about a subject on Thursday, I would set him up with a question during the Friday broadcast, then die as I heard him dismiss the topic. He apparently had changed his mind. It worked in the other direction as well. I carefully avoided talking about topic X, the subject for which he had shown no enthusiasm during the Thursday phone call, then in the middle of the Friday broadcast he would say, "You know, Colonel, what's really on my mind this week is topic X." Hello? What's that you say? He had changed his mind again. And since it was Red Barber, I couldn't get angry. In fact, it happened so often that Schramm and I would have a good laugh about it later. We still do.

Obituaries are what we did best. That was to be expected. It is a sad fact of an old person's life that he attends a lot of funerals. A great many of Red's friends and associates died over the twelve years of Red's broadcasts on NPR. Red gave many of them a great send-off. He was so good at obits that I regret he won't do mine. And it wasn't just the sports figures who got the treatment. As a celebrity, Red got to meet a lot of his contemporaries in other fields. His comments on the deaths of Ethel Merman and Fred Astaire ranked with those he made on the passing of Brooklyn's Boys of Summer.

If I could have more Fridays with Red, I would ask him fewer baseball questions and perhaps more questions about the jobs he had when he was working his way through college. One of his obituary writers said Red cleared the muck out of swamps. I didn't know that. That must have been when he worked for the highway depart- ment. Red's niece told me about the practical jokes played by Red's father. I would like to hear more about those. Red's sister, Effie Virginia, told me that Red used to bun- dle up their little brother, Billy, and pull him all over Co- lumbus, Mississippi, in a little red wagon.

Some early radio tales of producing programs at WRUF in Gainesville would be interesting. Radio was still in its first decade, and they were making it up as they went along. Having been there for NPR's early days, I know how exciting that can be. I would like to hear more about Red's days at WLW in Cincinnati, when most of the coun- try could hear Red's twenty-something voice hosting lots of programs that had nothing to do with sports. Like Red, a few of the singers and actors on those programs made it to the big time.

Why didn't I ask him about working with the big bands? The Depression was on. Nationally known radio figures like Red were among the few people with some money to spend. And there was Red with Woody Herman and Sammy Kaye, introducing the bandleaders and doing their Old Gold commercials. Sounds like heaven to me.

Still, it's difficult to have any regrets about the broad- casts we did, especially considering the reaction from lis- teners. The hundreds of "Dear Colonel" letters I received when Red died reflected the same sentiments expressed by listeners throughout Red's twelve years on *Morning Edi- tion:*

"I appreciated Red's ability to put the public spotlight

into perspective. . . . Unlike so many sportscasters and writers of today, he brought us the show—he never tried to be the show." **Billings, Montana.**

"I remember feeling how strange it was when I started to pay more attention to the magnolias than the sports talk. At some point, the commentaries became—as I found myself approaching middle age—an introduction to the idea that aging, rather than being something to fear, can be done with grace and joy. Red led me to realize that there simply wasn't any good reason to 'rage against the dying of the light.' What a wonderful lesson to learn and what an important time in my life to learn it." **Brooklyn, New York.**

"I looked forward to each week's conversation with suspense: what subjects will Red touch on today? I learned much more about baseball than I ever suspected there was to be learned, but I also picked up a lot about Florida's flora and fauna, and his spiritual outlook always made me remember my grandfather, the Southern Baptist Creek Indian, whose calm acceptance of the rhythms of life steady me to this day." **Ann Arbor, Michigan.**

"I was more often still in bed, counting my stiff joints and envying Red, who, in the same time zone, was already cheering his listeners, his civilized diction a pleasure to hear, despite one's degree of interest in the subject." **Wrightsville Beach, North Carolina.**

"Mr. Barber seemed to honor the past, to pass it on to us, and yet not to deify it." **Washington, D.C.**

"Before World War II and the advent of modern telecommunications, I was a very provincial Brooklynite. To me the South was the land of racist senators and a *Gone With the Wind* society. The Mason-Dixon Line was as impenetrable as the Berlin Wall. The voice of Red Barber was instrumental, however, in breaking this barrier. His Southern voice was full of compassion and decency. It had no bounds. When Red Barber solicited for blood donors during World War II, I realized that a bond of decency tied people of all cultures together. Red Barber was more than a ball and strike announcer. His was a voice which made walls tumble." **Rockaway, New Jersey**

"I am one of the many people who, on Friday A.M. at 7:35: [A] was never in the shower, [B] never taking out the trash, [C] never having a serious conversation with a wife, a lover, attorney, broker or car mechanic. I was listening to Red Barber on public radio. Finding him on the radio was a gift. Everything, the cats, the flowers, family comments, whatever, I wanted to hear from him. He was the most decent gentleman, and he always will be." **Brockton, Massachusetts.**

"He was my radio grandfather, telling me stories, charming me into a love of sports I hadn't expected." **Pennsylvania Furnace, Pennsylvania.**

"I could always depend on the wisdom and perspective of that old voice to tell a story that would bring some sanity to these times of folly and lack of spirit and concern for the great gifts of life. . . . It is ironic then, that I, a Black man, would find this man to be like the grandfather I never had. It was his wisdom and love of life that I will remember and revere and try to emulate." **Chicago, Illinois.**

"For many, many Friday mornings I heard my father in Red's gentle voice. Now that there will be no more talks with Red on my way to work, I think I really will have finally lost my father, who died a year ago." **Awendaw, South Carolina.**

"Red's commentary always reminded me of my daughter Meg when she first learned to walk. I had no idea where she was going or what she was going to do when she got there, but she was a pure delight to watch. So it was with Red." **Rochester, New York.**

"Though my husband and I don't recognize an umpire from a bat boy, we anticipated every Friday morning when Red Barber would talk to us of watermelons, weather and baseball. Our careers have moved us around the country, but on every Friday morning of our married lives, whether in Indiana, North Carolina, New York or South Carolina, one of us would look across the breakfast table and say, 'There's Red, thank God it must be Friday!' " **Columbia, South Carolina.**

"How nice to think we get the last day of the work week and Red Barber all in the same day! . . . I know I can call my mother in Tulsa, and we can talk to each other about Red. I can call my sisters in far-off places, but not so far that they don't get NPR, and we will talk about Red." **Portland, Oregon.**

"My father was raised in Mississippi. I grew up in north Jersey in the '50's; lived in Florida in my 20's, and now live in Kentucky. For five minutes each Friday, I was all in one place." **Lexington, Kentucky.**

"He crafted imagery for his audience. It was made up largely of first and second generation Americans 'from everywhere' and through his concise, understated accounts, he gave us a mythic grasp of another, more genteel America, courtly and steeped in arcane traditions. Through his reporting on the most American of pastimes, he helped all of us to be part of America, no matter where we started from." **Jamesburg, New Jersey.**

"His profoundly spiritual insight gave us the long view, reminding us that character is a virtue, that beauty can carry us through the day ('the camellias are blooming'), that good living is not about taking yourself too seriously, making a contribution, and certainly is about having fun and doing it with flourish and panache. Colonel Bob, I too feel like I never wanted this to end. I can only say that somewhere deep inside the memory of Red Barber brings me the smile of knowing that life can be well lived and made better by sharing its blessings." **Brooklyn, New York.**

Red with his little sister Effie Virginia and their baby brother Billy in Columbus, Mississippi, in 1915.

Milestones

FRANTIC COVERAGE of breaking events is the business of a news program. We do the best we can and hope it's good enough. But we also long to do stories more deliberately, stories that stand as radio art. Anniversaries are perfect for this. We can see them coming and plan for them. We can gather material, edit the tape, fine-tune a script, carefully narrate and package the story with some well-chosen music and other aural ornaments.

Red Barber was made for anniversaries. Much of his long career is on tape, and it's a rich archive. The dates were no problem; Red was a one-man calendar. January was the month he started on *Morning Edition*. February contained his birthday. March included his wedding anniversary and the date of his first radio broadcast. April had baseball's opening day, and Red broadcast his first major league game on opening day in 1934. Every month offered an anniversary. He was good for holidays, too, and every December he told us his Christmas story:

RED: Christmas is very meaningful to me. My dad was a locomotive engineer, but he never would go out on the road on Christmas Day. He always stayed home. And I've tried to follow that tradition. I know I did a dozen New Year's Day football games—one in New Orleans and two in Pasadena and nine in Miami—and always there was pressure to get you to come down early. But I never would go down until the day after Christmas. And I think it all goes back to Christmas in Columbus, Mississippi, in 1914. I was almost seven and my sister was almost five. We got up early on Christmas morning, and when we went in, all we could see was the Christmas tree and the fire in the fireplace, and my father was standing in front of the fireplace. And as small children are, we were completely greedy. We kept opening packages and playing with toys and this, that and the other. And it never occurred to me, certainly, to even ask my dad where my mother was. And we just kept going on our selfish ways.

And then, finally, I remember my father, and I remember the picture very well as he stood before the fireplace. He was wearing a corduroy suit. He said to my sister and to me, "Would you like to see *my* Christmas present?" And we said, "Oh, sure." So he took us by the hand and he took us into the front bedroom. And there in the bed was my mother. And with her was my little brother, Billy, who was born on Christmas Day, 1914. So, as you can see, this has always been a very meaningful day in this family, Robbit.

On February 19, 1982, I congratulated him on his seventy-fourth birthday, which had occurred two days earlier.

RED: Thank you and my friends at NPR for sending the dozen balloons. I didn't even know you sent out balloons before. And I thought it was very apt because when I was born seventy-four years ago, if you wanted to fly someplace, you *went* by balloon. I remember as a boy during the First World War, I used to run out into the street to see the first airplanes in that part of the country in Mississippi.

BOB: Somebody told me you had a newspaper from the day you were born.

RED: Yes. I'm looking at the front page of *The New York Times*, which I got some years ago. And the sports story on it—it's a full column—is about racing automobiles. And it tells the story of racing automobiles that went from Geneva, New York, to Buffalo, and I read now, "a distance of 119 miles." The first car covered it in seven and a half hours, and the second car, eight hours and forty-five minutes. What do you think of that, going back seventy-four years, for a speed on the road?

BOB: Really movin' along, weren't they?

RED: Well, they didn't have any paved roads then. They were just running in mud and snow and ice. Bob, when you think about it, we have been living in the most rapidly changing civilization in the history of mankind. Everything's changed, and changed so rapidly.

BOB: What else is in that paper, by the way?

RED: Well, one story is very interesting. It says, "No Gold Mines on the Isthmus—The Digging of the Panama Canal Is Not Going to Bring Us Riches." . . . There had been a rumor that as they were digging the Panama Canal, they had discovered gold, and that was going to make us rich. . . .

BOB: Keep going. This is wonderful. I'm enjoying this.

RED: Well, I know that Theodore Roosevelt was the president. As far as baseball was concerned, the Chicago Cubs had done that rare thing that they haven't done in modern times: they beat the Detroit Tigers in the World Series the fall before. Ty Cobb had won his first batting championship. Honus Wagner had won another one. And in the World Series, in 1907, . . . the total attendance was seventy-eight thousand people. The total winning share for each player was two thousand dollars, for the losing player about nineteen hundred dollars. . . . And as far as football goes, the champions of the Big Ten in 1907 and 1908 when I came along—the University of Chicago under Amos Alonzo Stagg. . . .

BOB: Any sage advice on your seventy-fourth birthday?

RED: Yes. I would just recommend to anybody who's listening to just do the best they can to make it.

Red's seventy-fifth birthday fell on a Thursday, and sports producer John Ogulnik made it a major production. There was tape of Red doing play-by-play, tape from interviews with Red, and testimonials—including this one from CBS chairman William Paley:

First on radio and then on television, Red helped to pioneer the development of that unique blend of journalism and art that sports broadcasting, at its best, represents. And millions of listeners still remember the excitement he brought to those wonderful summer afternoons when he transported us out to the ballpark. Red has given a lot of pleasure to a lot of people. And he is still doing so by virtue of his weekly appearances on National Public Radio. Many thanks, Red, and best wishes to you on this special day and for many, many more to come.

There were also birthday tributes from a couple of the Dodgers from Red's days in Brooklyn. Don Newcombe was one of the first blacks to join Jackie Robinson at Ebbets Field:

Red really got to the point where he didn't give a damn what color the guy was as long as he could play baseball for the Dodgers and he could sit up there and talk about him and admire him. And I remember Jackie saying years ago that Red was a gentleman and he always was in his corner and he could always depend on Red to give him the necessary backup he needed. And explaining to people what was going on on the field, people who couldn't see because there was no television at that time—they had to go by what Red was telling them, and Red told the people the truth. Jackie admired Red very, very much, as I recall. Oh, so do I. And Roy Campanella, also.

Pee Wee Reese was one of Red's favorites. He was the Dodger captain. Later, he became a broadcaster. Red campaigned for Reese to be enshrined at the Hall of Fame. Eventually, he made it.

Every time I think of Red Barber, I think of nothin' but class. Anytime that Red Barber's name is mentioned, I always recall the time when . . . Red [said], "There's a little fly ball hit in back of shortstop and Pee Wee Reese drifts back saying, 'I'll take all of these you can send me.' Oops, he dropped it." And they always kid Red about that, but he's a beautiful man. I had a chance to work with some of the really great announcers, like Jack Buck and Harry Caray. I never had a chance to do a ball game with Red Barber. He was always my favorite and I would have loved to have done a ball game with him.

We ended the segment with a live phone conversation with Red. But we weren't through celebrating his seventy-fifth. The next day was Friday, Red's regular day. I did not start the conversation with him until we played another testimonial obtained for us by then White House correspondent Jim Angle. It was a taped message from President Ronald Reagan.

Because I started out as a sports broadcaster myself, I remembered that yesterday was the birthday of one of America's greatest, Red Barber, the man who kept us on the edge of our seat every time a pitcher wound up and the batter stood at the plate with a full count. But Red Barber is not just an announcer. As he frequently reminds us, he is a sports reporter, bringing to his profession the highest journalistic standards. Red, back when you were the voice of the Cincinnati Reds, I was out in Des Moines calling the plays for the Cubs. I'll have to admit I was always a little in awe of the treasure chest of knowledge you brought with you to every game. You were a walking, talking sports encyclopedia. By the end of the ninth, the audience not only knew about the game, they had also been given a sports history lesson as well.

Your professionalism and, I might add, a personality that won't quit earns you the reputation of dean of sports broadcasting. And although I've gotten into a different line of work, I can still appreciate what you've done for the art. Yesterday, you were only seventy-five years old. So we're all looking forward to many more years of baseball insight. I want to thank Bob Edwards and the staff of *Morning Edition* for letting me be part of this tribute to a good friend and a great American, Red Barber.

Red was surprised and grateful, but certainly not speechless. In fact, he recalled when and where he and

Reagan first met—at the Edgewater Beach Hotel in Chicago in 1938 at a conference General Mills arranged for
baseball announcers. How *did* he remember things like
that?

Five years later, in February of 1988, it was Mark
Schramm's production that marked Red's eightieth birthday. The piece featured cats, camellias and Red's calls of
the Gionfriddo catch and a Tommy Henrich home run.
Then, there was this from Mel Allen:

> He has done things as a broadcaster that have helped young
> people. They look toward him to learn how to broadcast.
> And, in fact, there are professional broadcasters who have
> tried to copy, imitate, impersonate. But you can't do that to
> an original. And he is an original.

Next we heard from Vin Scully.

> He had the greatest influence on my broadcasting life of
> anyone in this world. He was like a second father to me. In
> fact, in looking back, there was a distinct and definite feel-
> ing of paternalism in our relationship. He was the older
> broadcaster and I was the kid. I guess if I had to sum up his
> relationship with me and why it was so important, I could
> sum that up in two words: he cared. He wanted me to
> succeed. And when it was all said and done, I think he
> accomplished his work. He was a remarkable man and I was
> much richer for knowing him.

Then, words from another former associate, Ernie Harwell.

> Well, I'm proud of Red reaching eighty. I think he was a
> real pioneer in our business, and I've got a great regard for
> him because I think he set the pace for just about everybody
> who followed him. He was a real professional. He was the
> first guy, I think, in baseball broadcasting who took it away
> from a guy just buying a scorecard and going to the ball-

park and broadcasting to really being a professional and going out and researching the teams, the players, the umpires, the managers and doing a real, top-notch reportorial job.

Ron Gabriel, president of the Brooklyn Dodgers Fan Club, said he thought Red's soothing, Southern tones helped Brooklyn fans keep the game in perspective and "prevented numerous ulcers and heart attacks."

Red had the last word. He had told me earlier that it was a piece of broadcasting advice given him by Arthur Godfrey.

It came to my mind as I would sit at the microphone doing baseball games: I'm going to tell this game to one person. And that's all I ever thought about. I thought about the one mike in front of me and thought about the one person who would be listening.

Red's tenth anniversary on *Morning Edition* in January of 1991 prompted another Schramm production with more highlights from Red's years on NPR and a bit of the *Symphony in D for the Dodgers*. The segment began with my asking Red if he was going to have a good weekend. He replied, "Bob, I'm superstitious to this extent: I make it my business to have a good weekend every time I run into one."

In February of 1991, I wished him a happy eighty-third birthday. He said, "Well, Colonel, I can just say with the writer of the Thirty-ninth Psalm, 'Spare me a little, that I may recover my strength, before I go hence, and be seen no more.'"

Colonel Bob on the left, NPR producer Mark Schramm on the right, stealing material from the *Tallahassee Democrat,* October 19, 1990. It was Schramm who kept the broadcasts going as Red's health was failing.

Partners

ONE FRIDAY, Red and I were in mid-conversation when suddenly the phone call to his house was disconnected. Listeners could hear Red, but Red couldn't hear me. Since we were "live" on the satellite, it would have been awkward for Red to put down the phone and wait for us to call him back. He also didn't want to leave me in the position of having to fill all that airtime. Instead, he acknowledged the problem to our listeners and continued talking about sports until his stopwatch told him it was time to stop. Our dialogue became Red's monologue. My mood went from shock over the technical glitch to astonishment over how lucky I was to be working with the consummate professional. Listeners probably "heard" me smiling as I thanked him and wrapped up the segment. A broadcasting legend had just said, "Excuse me, son, let me show you how this is done."

He was probably still in his twenties when he started calling himself "the Ol' Redhead." But if I had just once said, "Well, how's the Ol' Redhead?," I would have received a stern lecture from our politically correct listeners about the proper way to address "our senior citizens." Most listeners could tell that I loved the man. Some detected his regard for me. Former *Morning Edition* producer Jay Kernis said, "Red knew there was a Bob/Red relationship," and there was a certain warmth to Red that was lacking when he wasn't talking with me.

Red was great fun. The best laugh I got out of him had to do with the camellias, and of course he topped me right away. He was talking about gibbing, which is the process of accelerating the flowering time and enhancing the size of the blossom with gibberellic acid, a natural plant hormone. I had never heard of this before, but he plowed through that and had moved on to another subject when I said, "Gibberellic acid?" This really amused him for some reason. I guess he thought it was funny that this plant philistine was still back there on the peculiar word when he had moved on. So finally I had broken him up, but then he said, "Yes, and I could spell it too if we had more time."

It's impossible to determine whether two people are going to work well together. Fred Astaire had many partners. Why did the act play best when he was dancing with Ginger Rogers? Hard to say. Some of the others were probably better dancers, but it just wasn't the same.

That's the way it was with Red. I couldn't be there every Friday, and when I was away, Red's segment was an adventure. NPR has a special knack for hiring people who know nothing of sports. Some of my substitutes were not

familiar with the subject. Plus, they would have to deal
with Red's unpredictability, his change of mind about what
he wanted to discuss, and his love of spontaneous, ad-lib
broadcasting. Lots of NPR reporters can do this quite well
when the subject concerns their specialties, but this was
foreign territory. Sometimes Red would ask questions.
This is very awkward for reporters whose professional
training teaches them never to utter an opinion on any
subject beyond the weather. Some made the mistake of
thinking they were to interview Red. Red's segment was
not an interview, it was a series of questions or statements
designed to let Red run with the ball. And the substitute
hosts weren't always mindful of the conventions of Southern conversation. They didn't know where Red's periods
and commas were in his speech—much less his semicolons.
So there was cross talk, with the resulting "Oh, I'm sorry,"
or "No, you go ahead." Listeners mistook this for hostility
on Red's part, resentment that he had to talk with somebody other than the Colonel. That wasn't it at all. My colleagues were just as conscious as I was that the man from
Tallahassee was a broadcast legend, and they were more
than a little intimidated. It was years before I could pull it
off; my NPR brothers and sisters didn't have the benefit of
those years.

The substitute hosts were ambivalent about Red. Some
enjoyed the experience. Some have painful memories. All
of them are accustomed to being in control of an interview, but there was no chance of anyone controlling a
conversation with Red. So while Neal Conan called it "the
longest four minutes in show business," he also says his
grandchildren are not going to believe he talked with Red
Barber. David Molpus recalls that "no matter what subject
I was told we'd be talking about, we wouldn't." But he says
talking with Red was "thoroughly enjoyable," and he liked
how Red forced him to be natural and to think on his feet.
Alex Chadwick would ask Red the question he was told
Red would like to be asked, only to hear Red say on the air,

"Alex, I don't think anyone's really interested in that." He compared his encounter with Red to a tap dance in which he "would be watching the other guy to see what step we were on." Alex thought of Red as "a rascal," but one who "legitimized us." Alex was grateful that Red, coming from the earliest days of radio, thought it was worthwhile to talk with the young people on this relatively new non-commercial radio network.

John Hockenberry compared his Friday with Red to a trip he took to Yankee Stadium with his grandfather. He fondly recalls the weather, the subway, the hot dogs, his grandfather—everything about it except the game. Similarly, he has warm memories of talking with Red about flowers and about John's wheelchair, but he can't recall what sports they discussed.

Scott Simon, sometimes given to hyperbole, said to me, "He hated me, he only liked you." Scott said that he "prepared for Red more rigorously" than he prepared for his interview with Mother Teresa, but that talking to Red "was like trying to impress someone on a first date." Scott would inject some of his sports knowledge into the conversation and then hear Red pounce on the one fact Scott had gotten only half right. Renee Montagne would rehearse a sports question and then fear that Red's follow-up would reveal she had exhausted her knowledge of the subject. Renee was a National Merit Scholar in high school and *summa cum laude* at Berkeley; she's uncomfortable about not knowing things. She says no president could intimidate her in an interview, but Red made her feel "like an eight-year-old girl."

Scott believed that Red's control of the conversation extended to "working the clock"—using time the way a basketball team does to hold on to a lead; "He always made sure he got the last word." But Susan Stamberg also worked the clock when she talked with him; she just kept talking. Others developed defense mechanisms of their own. Lynn Neary noticed the crape myrtle was in bloom, so she successfully raised that subject with Red. David Molpus figured he could always buy another minute by asking, "So what else is on your mind this week, Red?"

The tape of one Dave Molpus interview with Red makes me laugh until I cry. It was Christmas Day. They exchanged Christmas greetings, and Red noted that both of them were from Mississippi. Then Red went into his annual Christmas story about his little brother, Billy, being born on Christmas Day in 1914. Dave countered with a joke. I have known David Molpus for more than twenty years; we went to graduate school together. His on-air personality is ultra-conservative. He is the solid reporter—lots of steak, no sizzle. You'll see Halley's Comet more often than you'll hear Dave tell a joke on the radio. Yet he told Red about being a child in Belzoni, Mississippi, and opening Christmas presents "under the grits tree." Red's response was "Uh-huh." I couldn't believe it. For the first time in his long radio career, David Molpus extended his broadcast personality beyond his "just the facts, ma'am" approach and Red cut him off at the knees. But it wasn't cruel, it was funny. And sometimes Red would say "Uh-huh" when he hadn't heard the previous remark and didn't know what else to say.

In fact, Red would make a game try at establishing rapport with my replacements. He would try to learn something about them, perhaps their hometowns or their areas of journalistic expertise. One of my favorite incidents occurred once when Cokie Roberts filled in for me. Cokie was prepared to talk about camellias, but Red asked her about her family instead. Then he asked her the question everyone asks when first meeting her. "What kind of name is Cokie? I knew a Cookie Lavagetto, but I've never known anyone named Cokie." They ended up talking about the issue of the Knute Rockne twenty-two-cent stamp just as the minimum rate on a first-class letter was moving to twenty-five cents. Cokie suggested the Postal Service issue

a Ronald Reagan three-cent stamp to make up the difference.

Cokie believes Red sincerely worried about me and
feared that I wouldn't return to the program. Alex Chadwick says listeners "could hear the disappointment in Red's
voice when the Colonel was absent." Neal Conan suggests
I was Red's security blanket. Neal says that when his father
reached a certain age, predictability became extremely important: "The grapefruit had to be sectioned just so, and
God forbid that you bought the large-curd cottage cheese."
He thinks Red had the same reaction when I wasn't there
on Friday. Producer Mark Schramm says Red was comfortable with me and trusted me.

We couldn't talk about basketball. I love it; he hated it.
We should have talked more about golf. I never played; he
did. He liked the fact that golf involves the individual alone
against other individuals, the elements, the course and his
own limitations. We never discussed boxing. We agreed it
should not be considered a sport.

Sometimes I could read his moods. Occasionally I could
tell when he wanted me to ask a follow-up. When I missed
the signal and moved on to another topic, he would hop
back to the previous one. Familiarity was no help then. But
I knew how to get a laugh out of the running jokes in our
routine. If he rambled on about cats and camellias, I would
say, "Yes, but how about those Dodgers?" He knew what I
was doing, though some of our listeners thought I honestly wanted to know about those Dodgers.

For some listeners, the partnership itself was what endured beyond the subject of the conversation. Here's what
they had to say when the dialogue ended:

"Perhaps, with Red and the Colonel, I could spend a few
minutes every Friday morning dreaming about how it
could be between my father and I and the game of baseball." **Bethesda, Maryland.**

"I am closer to his age . . . than yours . . . but I am happy to note that there is no generation gap between people whose culture, education and good manners are the same. . . . There was a magical chemistry to your friendship." **Indianapolis, Indiana.**

"For me, your conversations with Red Barber were the voices of father and son, whose evolution into friendship during middle/old age create some of life's best moments." **Sacramento, California.**

"Listening to you two talk about anything was like peering over the shoulders of two friends looking at photos both loved and enjoyed. Sharing in your friendship was a lovely gift." **York Harbor, Maine.**

". . . there was one more special tone in his voice that spoke to me as a father and grandfather. That nuance of speaking was the subtle pride that he must have felt in your accomplishments as a colleague and broadcast journalist not unlike that felt by every father in his son's or protégé's success and good works." **Reston, Virginia.**

"His love and respect for you also could be heard on these broadcasts. You were a good duet. . . . Red and the Colonel touched many of us. It's too late to tell that to Red, but it is not too late to tell you, and to thank you." **Brooklyn, New York.**

Red and Lylah in their backyard in 1992.

Lylah

I NEVER SAW RED BARBER ALONE. Lylah was always with him. She was at his elbow. When someone new approached, he would immediately introduce the person to Lylah. Periodically, he would ask her if she wanted something to eat or drink. It seemed that he was constantly looking after her welfare and happiness. I always thought this was the action of true love and a bit of guilt. He talked so often of the sacrifices she made and the loneliness she endured during his career that I figured he was trying to make up for it in retirement. I still think all that was true, but there was more.

It wasn't until Red died that I learned Lylah has Alzheimer's disease. He never mentioned it to me. He told me she wasn't doing well, and he told me about a terrible fall that she had. That information applies to a lot of women in their eighties. In recent years, my conversations with Lylah were brief. I would ask her how she was doing and she would say, "Mean as evah." Nothing there to indicate anything wrong. But by the time Red died, her condition had deteriorated far more than most people knew.

In the mid-1980s, Red told me he and Lylah were thinking of moving to a nursing home in Gainesville. According to Sarah, her mother's first symptoms appeared about that time. Sarah says her parents also looked at places in Jacksonville, Florida, and Charleston, South Carolina. But Lylah never found a place that was satisfactory to her, and Sarah suspects Red was never willing to give up his own privacy to live in a nursing home. So they decided to continue to enjoy their own home and garden and have as normal a life as possible. He would look after her for as much time as they had together. It was his final act of love. When he slipped into a coma in October 1992, he could no longer cover for her; the hospital staff suddenly realized that they received two patients when the Barbers checked in.

Back in 1985, when she was almost seventy-nine years old, Lylah's autobiography was published. We discussed it on *Morning Edition* on April 2.

BOB: Lylah Murray Scarborough was born in north Florida. Her father died when she was five and her mother moved to Jacksonville, where Lylah was raised

by an indomitable grandmother and her mother's sister, Aunt Ouida.

LYLAH: Aunt Ouida was just something special.

BOB: When she got to her third divorce, she had a wonderful line.

LYLAH: Yes. A young relative was bemoaning her second marriage that was failing and said, "But, Ouida, I
thought he was different." And Aunt Ouida with her
wonderful knowledge said, "All men are different. All
husbands are the same." But I tell you, when she died
after a lingering illness, two of the three husbands
came when she was still alive and ill to see her.

BOB: You had not the happiest of childhoods, though.
You had a stepfather you weren't terribly fond of, and
there was a boarding school that's straight out of—

LYLAH: Purgatory!

BOB: —I was going to say *Oliver Twist*, but—

LYLAH: That didn't last too long.

BOB: How did you decide to go into nursing?

LYLAH: I didn't. I came home my senior year in high
school, and there was a seamstress—whom I'd never
seen—busy making this white-and-blue-checked uniform. And I was told that I was going into Riverside
Hospital as a student nurse. But if I hadn't done that,
I wouldn't have met this wonderful man I've been
living with for fifty-four years.

After the obligatory biographical data about Red, I
asked if she ever felt as if she wanted to stand up and say,
"Hey, I know he's the celebrity, but I'm somebody, too."
Lylah said, "Now, Bob, why do you think at my age I sat
me down and wrote that book?"

BOB: Did you listen to the games in Cincinnati and New
York?

LYLAH: Oh, yes, always, because that was part of my job,

> I thought. I'd listen because I knew I would tell him
> the truth. I would not, for anything, be other than
> completely honest with him.

BOB: So at the conclusion of the 1966 season, when the
Yankees—by then owned by CBS—said to Red, "We
do not choose to renew your contract," what were
your feelings?

LYLAH: I was absolutely furious. I still am. I am this
morning as I talk with you, as I think of it. It was an
outrageous performance. To see a proud man so hu-
miliated and hurt.

She told me she critiqued his performance on NPR each
Friday, so I asked her how she felt he was doing. "It var-
ies," she said.

In the preface to her book, she wrote, "Did I wish to
even some long-standing scores? Yes. Writing is a kind of
therapy. It had done more to rid me of the Diocesan
School and of my stepfather than hours of psychoanalysis
did."

Lylah and two of her classmates were the first ever
awarded B.S. degrees in nursing at Florida State College
for Women. For whatever reason, the three were placed in
the School of Home Economics, where, among her
courses, was one called "Feeding the Family." Here's how
she told the story in *Lylah*:

> Every home economics major was required to take a semi-
> nar course her senior year. Each student presented an
> hour-long paper on a chosen topic. Can you imagine lis-
> tening to a solid hour on "Lace Making" or "Saving Steps in
> the Kitchen" when your degree was to be a B.S. in nursing?
> My hour finally came, and I presented a paper on "Diag-
> nostic Tests to Determine the Presence of Gonorrhea and
> Syphilis." This was 1929, and even the words were seldom
> spoken in polite society. I got my audience's attention.

In some ways, it was a mixed marriage. She showed up
for his sermons, but did not share his religious fervor. He

supported Goldwater, while she was an arch-liberal who felt Red's trip to Vietnam was giving support to the war. He was ever the smooth-talking Southern gentleman, while her idea of diplomacy was to bite her tongue. I don't think she bit it too often. But since both were independent types, each could admire that trait in the other. I would want them both on my side. As individuals, Red and Lylah were formidable. As a duo, they would have had no competition in the bantamweight tag-team mixed doubles.

They were partners for more than sixty-one years.

The Orange Grove String Band with their announcer and some-time vocalist in Gainesville, Florida, in the early 1930s.

Highlights

MORNING EDITION listeners have treasured certain Red Barber comments over the years, and not all of them fit the subjects of previous chapters. This chapter is devoted to collecting random moments from Red's commentaries over the years.

In April of 1981, *Morning Edition* provided live coverage of the first launch of the space shuttle. Neal Conan was our reporter at Edwards Air Force Base in California, assisted by former test pilot Chuck Yeager. Yeager's celebrity had been given a boost by Tom Wolfe's book *The Right Stuff,* but he was not yet the familiar figure of battery commercials on TV. There was quite a delay in the shuttle launch from Cape Canaveral, so I had lots of talks with Conan and Yeager.

April 10 was a Friday, Red Barber day on *Morning Edition.* When senior producer Jay Kernis, a native of Bergenfield, New Jersey, heard Yeager's West Virginia accent on his program, he decided Yeager should join Red for some serious vowel-stretching. I introduced them and let them go. Red, as always, found a common reference point for a chat with a stranger. He recalled that when he threw out the first pitch at Dodger Stadium, his catcher was Steve Yeager, the general's nephew. Yeager, now retired, remembered hearing Red when he was still a kid back in the mountains. So he asked, "Just how old *are* you, Red?"

When baseball owners fired Commissioner Bowie Kuhn late in 1982, Red gave me a rundown on every commissioner going back to Judge Landis, including the remark that, during his time in that post, Ford Frick slept as soundly as Rip Van Winkle. Since the job no longer meant anything, Red focused instead on something that endures.

RED: Last night, I went out to see and hear an opera that the School of Music of Florida State University put on, Mozart's *Così Fan Tutte.* And we think about these commissioners coming and going, all of these things like that, here's a piece of work that was written in 1788 and is still going strong. I think that's more important to think about this morning.

In June of 1983, *Morning Edition* had all of its commentators compose their weekly remarks as commencement addresses to the June graduates. Carl Kasell was filling in for me that day.

RED: I know that in the world of athletics that the athletes don't pay attention to gratuitous advice. The only time that an athlete will accept any advice is when he's in a batting slump or when he's in some sort of trouble and turns to his manager or his coach and asks for it. Actually, Carl, when you think about it, a graduation address comes a little bit too late. When you're speaking to students, you ought to start talking to them at the very early stages when they start going to school, because I think the mistake we make today is that we don't emphasize to our youngsters that going to school—getting an education—is their business. And it's a lifetime business, and it's very important. They should learn the value of work when they start to school. They should learn that going to school is the most important thing they can do. They've got to learn to read. If you can't read and you get out into the world—you in the pickle vat. Reading and writing are still the two basic tools.

And I think the respect for work is very important. I know that one of the most important things that was taught to me was—I had a professor that—he graded the class because you had to answer, in writing, a five-minute test on what was your homework every time you came in. And he taught me the importance of daily preparation. And I couldn't have done my broadcasts in the big leagues without doing daily preparation. I got that out of school.

I think it's important that we emphasize liberal arts today because, in addition to being able to earn a living, education should teach people that they will always have to live within themselves. Of course, I have a sort of hard-bitten attitude about education because I stayed out of high school two years before I went to college. And it took me two years of doing day labor, menial tasks, to understand that I really needed education.

On February 17, 1984, I congratulated Red on his seventy-sixth birthday and got a history of twentieth-century entertainment. He began with Ethel Merman, who had died that week at the age of seventy-five.

RED: She was a tremendous star on Broadway. She was always in a success; she never was in a flop. She made everything go. When Lylah and I first got to New York to do the Brooklyn Dodgers in 1939, the first Broadway show we saw was Ethel Merman and Jimmy Durante in *Stars in Your Eyes*. And I want to tell you that between Merman and Durante, there wasn't a quiet moment in the theater.

BOB: I'll bet! Well, we've talked about legends over the years in sports, and she certainly was one in the theater.

RED: Oh, yes. I've noticed that several of the stories have said that she was the greatest, the most dominant force that ever hit Broadway. I would say that she was one of the greatest, but not *the* greatest. Bill McCaffrey, my longtime friend and former agent, who started out in the days of vaudeville as Keith-Albee's office boy, knew them all. He's always claimed that the most dominant entertainer on Broadway was Al Jolson. And I know that I got to New York really too late. I saw Al Jolson in his last Broadway show. But then you think of entertainers who have made an impact in the country—this is before you were around—but Gene Austin sang "My Blue Heaven" in 1927. And this was before radio was effective, no TV, and suddenly he sold over two million copies of "My Blue Heaven" on records and they stopped counting. Nobody ever had a success like that. People used to wait for the latest Gene Austin record.

And, of course, along came Bing Crosby. And other singers that I have enjoyed so much in my leisure time when I wasn't working and when I wasn't around

sports, Robbit—John Charles Thomas; Richard
Tucker, an extremely versatile singer, opera as well as
popular. The versatile singer today is Placido Dom-
ingo. And one of the highlights, I think, for Lylah and
me as far as entertainers go, was opening night of
South Pacific, with Mary Martin and Ezio Pinza. Do
those names ring a bell?

Bob: Sure. You bet. I know a little something, you
know. You got to meet Merman, didn't you?

Red: Yes, Ethel Merman and I met in the reception
room. We had the same ear, nose and throat special-
ist, Dr. Stuart Craig in New York. He was a very gentle man and he used to take care of some of the big
performers. And Ethel Merman was always Ethel
Merman whether she was in the reception room or on
the stage. She was herself. She never took a lesson.
She was a natural.

Then I said goodbye, and our alert director was ready
with Merman singing "Everything's Coming Up Roses"
from *Gypsy*. Youuu'lll beee swell, you'll be great! She was.
And so was Red.

In June of 1984, Edwin Moses was going for his hun-
dredth consecutive victory in the four hundred meter hur-
dles. Red offered insight.

Red: Well, I think it's wonderful, not only the physical
ability, but it's very important to recognize that when
someone continues such a continuity of success, the
price they pay spiritually for, you know, continuing to
want it so badly that you continue training and stay in
condition and meet all competition.

Bob: Well, what do you mean, the price you pay spiritually?

Red: It's so easy when you win a few times, Bob, to then
begin to take it easy, to say, "Well, I just don't have to
get up that early tomorrow morning. I don't have to

train that hard." It is harder to continue at the top than it is to get there. When you're on your way, then, of course, the future is beckoning. You've got people ahead of you and you want to get rid of them. But to get on top and receive the adulation of the world and everybody wants to pat you on the back and this, that and the other, that's very hard. That's why you do not often see baseball teams repeat. I have wondered, seeing the terrible start that the championship Baltimore Orioles got off to this year, if, somehow during the winter, they didn't lose something in a spiritual way. That was a bad beginning for that ball club.

"It is harder to continue at the top than it is to get there." Our subject was Edwin Moses, but I got the feeling he was talking about Red Barber. Notice also the smooth transition from Moses to the pennant races. That's what broadcasters call a good segue. For all of Red's many talents, good segues were not among them. He usually resorted to the tired old phrase "and speaking of," as in "and speaking of baseball, Colonel, did you happen to see . . ." Lame, very lame. But he had one beautiful segue during which he nearly became Alistair Cooke. It occurred in July of 1984 as the Democratic party was making history with the first national ticket to include a female candidate.

RED: You know what I was thinking, Bob, all the excitement about Geraldine Ferraro, et cetera, et cetera, and they've got the British Open going on at St. Andrews?

BOB: That's right.

RED: Well, do you know that Mary, Queen of Scots, was an avid golf player? And when she was a girl and sent to France to be educated, she took the game of golf with her. And the young men who chased the ball were called, in French, c-a-d-e-t-s, *cadets*, but the French pronounced it "caddies." And that term came back with Mary when she came back to Scotland. And to this day the fellows who chase golf balls are called caddies. And when she became queen in 1542, she played golf openly and gave it her blessing. And it was in her reign that this famous old course, St. Andrews, was founded. So you see, we're just a few hundred years behind over here.

BOB: The things you can learn on public radio! Just extraordinary. I'm not a golfer, Red, but when I see St. Andrews, see that beautiful old course, it has a big attraction for me. It makes me want to go out and get a set of clubs.

RED: I would like to see it. I've never seen it. But I know that it is the shrine. And there are a lot of American golfers who'll make a trip just to get a chance, not only to see it, but to play the course. . . . And [Greg] Norman almost burned up the course yesterday.

This was the "Tinker to Evers to Chance" of Red's many commentaries. He went from Geraldine Ferraro to Mary, Queen of Scots, to golf to French *cadets* to caddies to Scotland to St. Andrews to the British Open in one seamless set of transitions. What's that you say about stream of consciousness? Hey, it worked, didn't it?

The historical perspective came naturally to Red. If he had a particular subject he wanted to bring to a Friday broadcast, he did his homework and came prepared. He was fond of quoting Casey Stengel, who would say, "You can look it up." Red looked it up. So we couldn't just discuss the 1984 Summer Olympics, we had to hear that "the first Olympics, because they became too professionalized, were banished by Emperor Theodosius the First of Rome around the end of the fourth century." If it was time for baseball's All-Star Game, Red was there with the history. The history of the baseball batting helmet was a good one, involving the effective end of Joe Medwick's career. I remember Red saying that the macho baseball players were reluctant to wear helmets until Ted Williams put one on.

Red had more to say about great performers. We began 1985 with Red telling me he was a little sleepy because he had stayed up late the night before watching Leontyne Price's farewell performance of *Aida* on PBS. He said it was magnificent and added that *Aida* is not grand opera, it's *grand* grand opera. When Eugene Ormandy died in March, Red told us that Ormandy was his favorite conductor, especially when the Philadelphia Orchestra was playing Tchaikovsky, Red's favorite composer. So when word came that Ormandy had died, Red and Lylah turned on the stereo and played Tchaikovsky's sixth, performed by the Philadelphia Orchestra with Ormandy conducting.

On January 2, 1987, Red announced that the previous day he had had a bowl of hopping john, a Southern delicacy of black-eyed peas and ham hock that is eaten on January 1 to bring good luck in the New Year. He also said Lylah had given him a new electric typewriter for Christmas and he intended to use it to write another book. I never heard another word about that book. Then I asked him if he'd made any New Year's resolutions. He said no, but he did have a thought to share, a quote from Victor Hugo written more than a hundred years ago: "Have courage for the great sorrows of life and patience for the small ones. And when you have laboriously accomplished your daily tasks, go to sleep in peace. God is awake."

Former Dodger Babe Herman died at age eighty-four late in 1987 and Red was in prime storytelling form.

RED: When you think of Babe Herman, you think of three men on one base, at third base. This happened back in 1926 at Ebbets Field. And Babe Herman has been the sort of fellow who's always been given a bad rap. They said he hit into a triple play. Well, it wasn't a triple play, it turned out to be a double play. The story on that, Bob, was that three men were on base and one man was out when Babe Herman came to bat.

And he hit a screaming, savage line drive off the concrete nearby right-field wall, and he took off. The
runner who was at third base, Hank DeBerry, scored.
Dazzy Vance, the Brooklyn pitcher that day, a big,
lumbering fellow, was down at second. He came on
down to third base and turned and started toward
home plate. And for some reason or other, as Dazzy
said, he just got a little conservative. He told me about
this. And he went back to third base. Well, Chick Fewster, who had been the runner at first, came sliding
into third. And Herman, who had his head down and
was running for all he could get, before anybody realized it he had come sliding in in back of Fewster. So
suddenly there were three runners on one base. Well,
the Boston Braves' infielders, they just started tagging
everybody, and the umpires called two of them out.
At Brooklyn they used to say, "Well, the Dodgers have
got three men on base." And the answer would be,
"On which base?"

BOB: According to *The Complete Dodgers Record Book*, it
says in this article, "The Babe played first base and the
outfield with equal disregard for his own safety and
the art of fielding." He had a little trouble with fly
balls.

RED: . . . People said he had a fly ball hit him on the
head. Babe told me that it never, never happened. He
said it came close one time. One hit him on the shoulder. He was sort of a gangly fellow. But he could hit.
And this is what I mean, that things never seemed to
go right publicly for Babe Herman. One year, 1930,
he hit .393. That's a lot of hitting, isn't it, Bob?

BOB: But he didn't win the batting title.

RED: No, he didn't, because Bill Terry hit .401. . . . Babe
Herman hit .324 lifetime. He hit the first home run
that was ever hit in a night game, out at Cincinnati. He
was a tremendous fellow, and a very pleasant, very
agreeable man to be around. But the onus on that

three men on third base should be on Dazzy Vance, not on Babe Herman.

My wife, the former Sharon Kelly, turned forty on June 19, 1990, and we splurged on a trip to Ireland so she could be out of the country for the ignominious occasion. Red told me I wouldn't have to kiss the Blarney Stone, so we skipped County Cork. I think Red meant that I already had the gift of gab. Sharon believes Red was saying I already was full of blarney.

From time to time, Red and the rest of the audience could tell that I had a cold. On those occasions, Dr. Barber would give me his prescription: a pair of clean, white sheets. He wanted me to rest.

On the last broadcast of 1990, I asked him if he and Lylah were going to have a little New Year's toddy. "No, Colonel Bob," he replied, "I'm just going to remember about the New Year what Lylah's cousin Eula used to say: 'Do a little plowin' every day, 'cause if you stop, you're a goner.' "

A number of no-hitters were pitched in 1991, but once again, Red put things into perspective. He told us the story of Bobo Holloman. "In 1953, he was a rookie pitcher with the then St. Louis Browns. And in his first start, he pitched a no-hitter. And then he never pitched another complete game. He only won two more games that season, and then he was gone. So that's the importance of no-hitters."

In July of 1991, he gave us another interesting bit of trivia. We were observing the forty-fourth anniversary of Larry Doby's becoming the first black player in the American League, which took some of the pressure off Jackie Robinson and Branch Rickey, who had integrated major league baseball a few months earlier. Red told us that Rickey was nervous about having "too many" black players. Don Newcombe and Roy Campanella were valuable farm-team players destined to join the Dodgers soon. Rickey was looking for another major league owner to take

some of the burden from him. It turned out that Rickey
also had the rights to Larry Doby. So he offered Doby to
Bill Veeck, then owner of the Cleveland Indians, provided
Veeck would put Doby on the Cleveland roster right away.
Red said that, to his knowledge, Doby was the only ball-
player Rickey ever gave away.

A week later, we talked about Marvin Miller's book, *A
Whole Different Ball Game.*

RED: ... Marvin Miller, since he took over creating a
    union for the ballplayers in 1966, has become since
    then the single most important man in baseball, and
    maybe in all sports.

BOB: The minimum salary when he took over was six
    thousand dollars. Today it's a hundred thousand.

RED: That's right. And under the Players Association,
    which Marvin Miller single-handedly put together and
    held together, we have arbitration, we have free
    agency, we have agents who can deal with the owners,
    we have this money that you spoke about. I know that
    in your work with the American Federation of Tele-
    vision and Radio Artists, you well know the impor-
    tance of a union. Our job in radio and television
    wouldn't be worth it without our union.

BOB: Baseball as it was when Miller took over, took over
    the Players Association, was really a plantation. The
    workers ... had to do whatever management told
    them to do and they had no other option.

RED: They had one option. A ballplayer had one option
    before Miller took over and formed the union. He
    could take finally what the owners were willing to of-
    fer or he could get out of baseball.

BOB: He had to play for whatever team baseball de-
    cided he should play.

RED: That's right. And that went for life.

BOB: And the courts and Congress routinely upheld
    baseball when matters went there.

RED: Oh, the silliest thing the Supreme Court ever did was when . . . [it] claimed way, way back yonder that baseball was not a business, that it was a game.

BOB: Although they feel that football is a business. That's the interesting contrast.

RED: I know. Our Supreme Court, Robbit.

BOB: Marvin Miller says that he got a lot of help from the people with whom he was negotiating because they were simply inept. He's particularly harsh on Bowie Kuhn, the former commissioner.

RED: This is a remarkable book because this is a remarkable man and his achievements are remarkable. And he calls all the shots. He doesn't cover up anything. He says exactly what he thought then and what he thinks now.

In April of 1992, there were a couple of nasty collisions on baseball fields. I asked Red how he handled news of injuries when he was broadcasting a game.

RED: . . . My philosophy was to remember that . . . the ballplayer's family, especially his wife, probably was listening. And I wanted to do everything I could to reassure her and the family that things were going along all right. I wanted to remind them that it was a book rule that they had to be—for example, a hit batter had to be taken off in an ambulance and a stretcher, that that didn't mean too much. And I would watch for the player's movements, and any little helpful sign that I could give, I would try to give it to the family. And I know that some ballplayers' wives have said, "Well, you know, I thought Red was talking to me." Well, I certainly was.

We were in our final season together, and I thought these broadcasts were some of our best. We said farewell to Eddie Lopat, Sandy Amoros and Billy Herman. We dealt with baseball's "Japan crisis," in which the president of Nintendo was part of a group buying the Seattle Mariners. Red recalled his six trips to Japan, where he witnessed the Japanese fanaticism about the game. Red noted that I was to throw out the first ball at a Tigers game in the stadium where Red broadcast his first World Series. He did a nice birthday salute to Pee Wee Reese. In September, I mentioned that the big news of the week was the establishment of the Tallahassee Sports Hall of Fame with Red Barber as one of the first inductees. Red was quick to respond that "I wouldn't be there except for this program, I'm sure." Let it not be said that Red's sense of humor faltered in his final weeks.

On September 18, Red noted that his daughter, Sarah, had been born fifty-five years ago the previous day. Sarah heard this as she was driving across the desert in New Mexico. Then I asked Red about a massive new coffee-table book titled *Golden Years of Baseball*. Red had written the book's foreword, a wonderful essay about the five or six men who, according to Red, had changed baseball. This was a perfect topic for a four-minute radio talk, so Red and I discussed the changes made to the game by Judge Landis, Babe Ruth, Larry MacPhail, Branch Rickey, Jackie Robinson and Marvin Miller.

Just five weeks later, after the funeral, Sarah and I were rummaging through Red's study, where he did the NPR broadcasts and where he kept up a massive correspondence right to the end. She noticed a stack of these big books and wondered why Red had so many. I reminded her that this was the book for which Red had written the foreword—the book we discussed on the day Red mentioned her birthday. She looked astonished and said, "When did he find time to do this?"

The End

TWO YEARS BEFORE HE DIED, Red sent me a note thanking me for a magazine profile I had written about him. He said he looked forward to each Friday spot with me. He said, "It keeps me going." I believe it did keep him going, but the going was tough.

The last years of Red Barber's life were hell. I did not fully appreciate that until he was gone. I didn't want to think about him as a sick person. I didn't want to face the inevitable. Obviously, I knew from the beginning that someday I would have to say goodbye to Red, and I never dreamed we would get nearly twelve years together. I think the longer he endured, the more health problems he defeated and the more I began to think he was immortal. Maybe our Fridays could go on and on.

In May of 1992, Red had cataract surgery. He was nearly blind by that time. He could make out a headline, but not much more. The cataracts had prevented him from properly preparing for his broadcasts. He was deaf in one ear, hard of hearing in the other and nearly blind. Lylah had become progressively more ill and caring for her was a great burden. When the cataract surgery failed, Red told his daughter, Sarah, he thought he would have to stop the broadcasts. He wanted to do them well or not at all.

Despite everything, he *was* doing them well. Many of the chats we had in that last year ranked with the best. Red's secret weapon was NPR producer Mark Schramm, who was doing a lot of research for him and bringing him up to date on current events. The other factor, of course, was Red's determination to answer the bell for the next round. Battling through his infirmities, taking care of a terribly ill Lylah and soldiering on with the broadcasts, Red was a study in courage in his final months.

On Friday, September 25, 1992, he was as sharp as ever, and we covered a lot of ground. I began by noting that the week had produced an unassisted triple play and that previously there had been only nine of those in history. Schramm briefed him well here. He came right back at me with the fact that two of the nine occurred on consecutive days in 1927. We discussed another firing of a baseball manager, the prospect of the San Francisco Giants moving to Florida, the Cubs dropping their challenge to National League realignment, the National Football League losing another free agency case, the sacking of Fay Vincent as commissioner of baseball and the return of Ernie Harwell to the broadcasts of Detroit Tigers games.

On the next Friday, October 2, Red told us it was getting "a little chillsome" in Tallahassee, and when he spoke it sounded as though he had a cold. He acknowledged that, and I told him to take care of himself. We discussed the race in the American League East, where Toronto was leading Milwaukee by two games. We laughed about George Brett getting picked off at first base after his three thousandth career hit. Red said it was understandable if Brett was distracted. Then we talked about three bits of baseball history that occurred in the first week of October: Bobby Thomson's 1951 homer, Roger Maris's sixty-first homer of the 1961 season and the alleged "called shot" by Babe Ruth in 1932. He was sharp on the details of all three events. I thanked him, told him I would talk to him the next week and again urged him to "take care of that cold or whatever it is." He said, "Okay, buddy." It was our final conversation.

On October 8, Schramm placed the routine Thursday call to Tallahassee. Red sounded no better than he had the previous week. He said that he had a sore throat and he didn't feel up to a broadcast the next day. I wasn't too worried. He had sounded mentally strong the week before and the usual little chuckles were there. This didn't seem nearly as serious as the time in the mid-eighties when I'm certain Red was convinced he was dying. He had gone into the hospital with, I was told, some sort of bladder infection. Yet he ended up doing the Friday broadcast from his hospital bed. For many months after that, he devoted his Friday chats to reflection. The Psalms came more frequently. Then, one day, he just snapped out of it and was more chipper than ever.

On Friday, October 9, when it came time to introduce Red, I told listeners he was not feeling well, and I pointed out that it was only the third or fourth Friday Red had missed in his twelve years on NPR. I further noted that the rest of us had missed a lot more than that. Yes, I played it down. Whatever it was, I was certain he would beat it. We were later to learn that on this day he calmly took care of his final business. He summoned his daughter, Sarah, from Santa Fe. He drove himself and Lylah to the hospital in the green Mercedes. He had himself admitted. Then he went into a coma.

On Saturday, Red underwent surgery to remove a bowel blockage. The surgery was successful, but the patient remained unconscious.

Schramm gave me the news on Red's condition on Monday. I had spent the weekend thinking Red had a sore throat, and suddenly I was hearing that I probably never would speak with him again. One of the cruel but strangely comforting elements of broadcasting is that it doesn't allow much time for mourning; there are plans to make and obituaries to prepare. Schramm was on temporary duty in our Chicago bureau, producing stories on the presidential election. Tom Goldman was producing sports out of Washington. I was due to leave in a week for a speaking engagement at Oregon State University in Corvallis. Schramm and Goldman remained in telephone contact with Sarah Barber in Tallahassee.

The Associated Press learned that Red was in the hospital. The AP reporter wanted a statement from me. For the first time in my life, I ducked a reporter. I've always felt everyone in our business has a moral obligation to help a fellow reporter on deadline, provided that reporter isn't in direct competition on a story. I didn't want to stiff the AP, but I also didn't want to have to make any statement that would bury Red before his time. I just said that Red was in our prayers. I did, however, prepare a statement to be released by NPR's Public Information Department if and when the end came:

> Red Barber's many accomplishments are well documented. He was a broadcast pioneer who set the standard for sports broadcasting. Most achievements in broadcast sports journalism were done first and done best by Red Barber. Few men in any field have contributed more to the English language. He was also a deeply spiritual man who never let our games or athletes have more importance than the wonders of God and nature. He was grateful to Jackie Robinson for helping him to confront racism and follow his conscience. He was proud of his service during World War II blood drives and morale-boosting trips to Vietnam. And few knew that Red Barber struggled with severe hearing impairment through most of his career.
>
> It has been my great joy to speak with Red every Friday on *Morning Edition* since January of 1981. Red was more important to the popularity of the program than any other individual. NPR stations knew better than to pre-empt Red for fund-raising drives, for fear of being swamped with protest calls from listeners. On a personal level, I don't know why Red took a liking to me, but it was clear that he did. Returning that affection was the easiest thing in the world. He was more than a mentor—he was a surrogate father. I loved him dearly and Fridays will never be the same.

On Friday, October 16, I told our listeners that Red remained in critical condition and that any cards or messages should be sent to *Morning Edition* for forwarding to the Barber family.

The following Tuesday, Tom Goldman produced an obituary for my narration. Both he and Mark Schramm were urging me to do a second piece, something more personal. I thought of the last line first. Once I started, I worked rapidly. The words flowed and so did the tears. I was done in just a few minutes and didn't change a word. Recording it, I didn't choke until the end. There were now two Red Barber farewells on the shelf ready to go. I left for Oregon hoping both pieces would stay on that shelf and collect dust.

The World Series has been played eighty-nine times. Baseball's premier event was only slightly older than Red. The eighty-ninth was being played while he slept.

On Thursday, October 22, Mark Schramm called me in Oregon and said, "I'm afraid the Ol' Redhead didn't make it." It was late in the morning. *Morning Edition* got the story into its final newscast. Our afternoon call-in program, *Talk of the Nation,* devoted one of its hours to Red. Robert Siegel was hosting that day and interviewed Robert Creamer, who had helped Red write his second book, *Rhubarb in the Catbird Seat.* Tom Goldman did a nice report that night for *All Things Considered.*

The next day was Friday, our day, and I was still in Oregon. Susan Stamberg hosted *Morning Edition.* Our obituary ran in the first hour. It began with my saying that Red was survived by his wife, his daughter, and millions of fans who loved his broadcasts and regarded him as someone very special. It ended with Red's recitation of the Thirty-ninth Psalm. And in the second hour, in Red's regular spot, listeners heard the eulogy I had left behind.

Every Friday, this segment of *Morning Edition* belonged to Red Barber. And with his death this week in Tallahassee, we turn the page on the best story in our radio magazine. One of the great voices of America will speak to us no more, and somehow the camellias will never smell as sweet. What to say about a man featured in a symphony and immortalized in a James Thurber story? Each conversation revealed a new dimension to the man. There was the baseball Red, the broadcasting Red, the gardening Red and the spiritual Red. We did a talk show once and a listener wanted Red to recommend some reading material. I was certain the question pertained to sports books. But Red's recommendations were *The Book of Common Prayer* and Winston Churchill's *History of the English-Speaking People.*

Red loved opera. In their New York years, he and Lylah had season tickets to the Met. And what a tragedy that severe hearing impairment in the second half of his life prevented him from enjoying his collection of opera records. Opera was our subject on a Friday or two. So were the cats and the camellias. Ultimately, we'd get back to baseball and the character of the people involved in the game. There's so much I've wanted to ask him these past few weeks. How would he feel about a Canadian team in the World Series? What about Cincinnati manager Lou Piniella voluntarily leaving a franchise he took to World Series victory just two years ago? I'd love to hear Red comment on that. But I won't. A listener wrote—too late—wanting Red to describe the one major league instance of an unassisted triple play by a first baseman. I'm sure Red would have had a reply. In speaking of Red, I often was tempted to say that Red had forgotten more baseball than anyone else knew. But it wasn't true. Red hadn't forgotten anything. I once had the bittersweet experience of following Red onstage before hundreds of Floridians. Red re-created from memory the ninth inning of the fourth game of the 1947 World Series. Red pointed out it was the first Fall Classic to be televised. It was the first to have six umpires, and Red named them all. He set the Yankee defense and called the play-by-play as if it were live. And for all of us listening, it was. This was the game in which Yankee pitcher Bill Bevens took a no-hitter into the ninth, only to lose the game because of a Dodger pinch hitter in his final season. And by the time Red had Lavagetto sliding into second after doubling in the tying and winning runs, people who had never seen a ball game were on their feet cheering, and old folks were rattling their walkers in appreciation. The audience was in no mood to receive the next speaker mumbling something about his subject, the First Amendment. I was a goner before I reached the podium.

Red Barber taught three generations of broadcasters. Are the students up to passing on the lessons? He taught us respect for the listener, respect for the language and respect for the truth. To Red, it was journalism, not just entertainment. He taught us when to speak and when to shut up, when to seize the microphone and when to let the game take over. Who will teach us now? I know that's not the right attitude. I know I should be celebrating the fact that a good man was given eighty-four years to share with us. And I know that Red would reach back to the Old Testament to tell me that this is the way it's supposed to be—that we're only here for a time. We make the most of it and then we move on.

But I feel cheated. There's so much more I need to know. And that's one of the more enduring Barber legacies—the notion that whether one is forty-five or eighty-four, the education continues. A man who remembered when airplanes and automobiles were new inventions found some new marvel every day. I'll try to hold onto that. That and the audio tape, for listening to that voice was better than a julep on Derby Day. Thanks, Red. And farewell, old-timer. The Colonel says goodbye.

Red in his beloved garden.

Brookmont Drive

MARK SCHRAMM, Tom Goldman and I shared a flight to Tallahassee on Sunday, October 25, 1992. We arrived at the Barber home in mid-afternoon and received the warmest of welcomes from Sarah. All three of us had talked to her on the phone, but we had never met her before. She wasn't hard to spot because she looked like the grown-up version of her photographs in *Lylah*. On a counter in the kitchen were about fifteen bottles of booze. "Here," she said, "help us empty Daddy's liquor cabinet." It looked as though Red had prepared for any eventuality. Irish wakes always have been my favorites. I poured the Old Grand-Dad, pointing out to my NPR buddies that the fellow on the label was Basil Hayden, and that his brother William was a direct Kentucky ancestor of mine. They made a game try at feigning interest. Well, Red would have liked the story.

We met nieces, nephews, cousins, neighbors and old friends. They treated us as if we had been part of the Barber family all of our lives. It was a great group and everyone had stories to tell. Red had left us all with lots of memories. But the best storyteller was Effie Virginia Wynne, Red's eighty-two-year-old sister. When Goldman heard her talk, he wanted to give her Red's old Friday spot on *Morning Edition*. Her first words to me were "So, you're the Kuh-null?" When I wrote this book, I asked her for stories about Red. She told me that all the good ones were too personal. "But you don't think *any*thing's too personal, do you, Kuh-null Bob?" That Effie's a smart one.

Sarah gave the NPR trio an assignment: we were to be the official escort for Mel Allen. We were proud to do it. Mel arrived in Tallahassee in the early evening, just about the same time his luggage was arriving in Orlando. He spent the rest of the night and early the next morning trying unsuccessfully to get the airline to reunite him with his belongings. We picked him up at his hotel on Monday morning, October 26, and drove him to the Barber home, where Sarah was delighted to see him. Then it was time to go to church. On the way, Mel told us about the last time he and Red had worked together. Cable TV mogul Ted Turner, owner of the Atlanta Braves, hired Mel and Red to broadcast a Little League World Series championship game in the late seventies. Mel recalled a photograph of the two of them interviewing the coach of the team from

Taiwan. He said the two broadcasters looked as intense as if they were doing a Yankees/Dodgers Series from the old days.

The weather was as beautiful as the best Tallahassee day Red ever described on *Morning Edition.* The service at St. John's was an Episcopalian classic. Red would have loved it, since it came from his beloved *Book of Common Prayer.* The opening hymm was "Joyful, Joyful, We Adore Thee." There was a reading from Isaiah, then Psalm 121—"I will lift up mine eyes unto the hills; from whence cometh my help." Next, came a reading from Romans and Psalm 23— "The Lord is my shepherd; I shall not want." After a reading from the Gospel of John, we stood and sang "Amazing Grace." There I was, a onetime Catholic altar boy, standing next to the former Melvin Israel, and we're belting out Protestantism's greatest hits! The eulogy was read by Dr. Stanley Marshall, the former president of Florida State University.

> He set new standards for speaking the language of sport. He spoke clean, uncluttered prose that cut to the heart of the action like a surgeon's scalpel. On Friday mornings for the past twelve years, the Old Redhead—that voice, the voice with the lyrical, transportational qualities—took us back to long-ago summers in our mother's kitchen, or on the back porch steps or in the family car with the windows down. The sounds and sights of Ebbets Field were palpable. If Red Barber had not emerged, he would have had to be invented. His meticulous preparation, his self-assurance, his sense of what a baseball broadcaster should be and do, and should not do, provided a sense of direction to this new branch of journalism. In this, Red's effect on his craft has been profound and lasting.

Then followed the Apostles' Creed, some more prayers, a blessing and "A Mighty Fortress Is Our God."

We filed out of the church and greeted our fellow mourners. Peter O'Malley was there representing the

Dodgers. I think both Red and Lylah wished their relationship with Peter's father had gone better; they liked
him better than Red liked working for him. Former Dodgers Ralph Branca, Duke Snider and Pee Wee Reese were
there. After all these years, I finally met Pee Wee, my
fellow Louisvillian, my fellow Colonel. Vin Scully was
there, too, thanks to a World Series victory by the Toronto
Blue Jays. If Atlanta had won another game, extending
the Series, Scully, working the game for CBS Radio, would
not have made it to Tallahassee. I had never before walked
out of a church and been asked to give an interview; on
this day, I gave a dozen. Then we drove Mel back to his
hotel and said goodbye.

The Reverend Dr. W. Robert Abstein was with Red's
family, waiting for us when we arrived back at the Barber
home. We went into the backyard to a spot in the middle
of five camellia plants. There was a pile of red clay about
a foot high. Next to that was a hole some eight inches in
diameter. Inside the hole were the ashes of Red Barber. I
needed anchoring, so I planted my left shoulder against
one of those tall, sheltering pine trees. Sarah dropped
some blossoms into the hole. Reverend Abstein suggested
we might want to participate in the service by taking a
handful of dirt and putting it on Red's ashes. No one
moved. He looked right at me and said it again. I went up
and put some clay back into the ground. No one else
moved. I don't know if the others were lost in their
thoughts and prayers, or maybe they just didn't want to
return Red Barber to the earth. Reverend Abstein ges-
tured for others to come forward. Finally, they did, one by
one. And it was over.

In the finest of old Southern traditions, the house was
filled with food of all kinds. I assembled a sandwich and
had a generous slice of Mississippi mud cake. It's one of
those heavenly confections that makes you feel the blood
rushing up to your face. There were more stories and
memories exchanged. Schramm spent about an hour in

Red's study, staring at the desk where Red sat and did his broadcasts for *Morning Edition*. The Electro-Voice 635A microphone appeared to be waiting to carry its master's voice. Red always saw that relationship the other way around; he said that being fired by the Yankees meant he "was no longer a slave to a microphone."

Sarah joined us and gave us sheets of paper from Red's personalized notepads. She gave Tom Goldman and me some of Red's books. My copies contained notes Red had made for sermons and speeches. I sat in Red's chair (the catbird seat?) and looked down at the desk-blotter-style calendar. Some of the days of October bore notes in his handwriting. I looked at October 22, the day he died. The next day was a Friday, our day. In the space for Friday, October 23, I wrote him a note. I wrote that I loved him and missed him and wished he were there.

Also at the house that day were Gene and Mary Louise Ellis of Tallahassee Nurseries. They gave Schramm, Goldman and me each our own camellia plant. Gene said he was sure Red would have wanted each of us to have one. We agreed. The plants, including roots, were about two feet high and weighed ten pounds each. They were wrapped in plastic. The three of us, in our best funeral clothes, toted these plants through airports in Tallahassee, Charlotte and Washington, D.C. It must have been quite a sight. Each of us had a coat or some carry-on items in one hand, the awkward plant clutched in the other arm, and we were talking to one another through the leaves. I personally planted what is now the official Red Barber camellia in the Edwards backyard. And, Red, I even know its name. It's a Lady Vansittart. And it will always remind me of you.

Tribute

TALLAHASSEE HONORED Red with a camellia garden in the city's McCarty Park. It's a fitting memorial to a man who told the world of Tallahassee's beauty.

One Tallahassee resident sent me a photo of a sign he nailed to a telephone pole in front of a popular breakfast spot in town. The sign said: So Long Red, 1908–1992.

The technicians at NPR kept Red's Friday satellite time marked on their logbook until the end of 1992. Next to Red's entry each Friday morning was the word "cancelled."

Sarah Barber returned Red's microphone and it will have a place of honor at NPR in Washington, D.C. The *Morning Edition* Red Barber/Bob Edwards baseball cap became a hot item. NPR's marketing division brought it out as a station premium just months before Red died.

Many letters of condolence addressed to *Morning Edition* were packed up and sent to Sarah. The ones addressed to me are bulging from three large folders. Most were addressed to "Colonel Bob." One was sent to "The Colonel, NPR, Washington, D.C." It got there. I stopped counting them when the volume reached five hundred and others were arriving. I have read and kept every one.

The mayor of Charleston, South Carolina, wrote to me. So did the president of the Texas League. There was a letter from Powel Crosley V, whose great-grandfather owned the Cincinnati Reds when Red became their radio voice. But most of the letters were from listeners hoping to ease my pain. They sensed my friendship with Red was such that I would need comforting. They were right about that. But I got the impression that they were working through their own grief by writing to me.

Those letters are the reason I wrote this book. I knew that Red was the most popular figure on any NPR program, but I didn't know that his death would cause our listeners to grieve so deeply. They didn't just write, they mourned. They told me what they were doing when they heard the news. They cried over the breakfast table. Some were still in bed and had trouble starting their day with such sad news. Quite a few were in their cars and had to pull over to the side of the road to regain composure. Many called their relatives in search of emotional support. One listener cried at a dinner party that night.

Listeners sent poems, essays and Bible verses. Those who had met Red described the encounters and the kindnesses he extended. He had signed their baseballs, autographed their books, answered their letters, consoled them in their hours of spiritual need and traded gardening tips with them. To those he hadn't met, it was a radio relationship—but one like no other. He was a stranger to no one who heard that soothing voice. His charm cut through the radio waves to every corner of America and touched people's hearts. We could not be the same after we heard him.

A few touched on something I could not ignore. "We shall rely on you to become the relay runner, catching his baton and winning the race," wrote a listener from Poughkeepsie, New York. Another, in Media, Pennsylvania, noted that "he became, in at least some ways, your mentor. He's gone, you're on your own, but you're not the same man you were before Red. . . . You will continue to grow."

Elliott Brack began his letter to me, "You were given this gift. . . ." Brack is with the Atlanta newspapers and he was encouraging me to write a book. "You have more work to do," he wrote. He was right about the book, obviously, and he was right about the gift, by which he meant my relationship with Red Barber. It *was* a gift, the perfect present to a man in mid-life and mid-career. It was a gift so grand that I hadn't known I needed it. Twelve years of conversations with Red reminded me of what is important and not important in sports, broadcasting, journalism and life. I've written as much as I remember, though I'm sure circumstances in the future will jog a memory or two that I'll wish I had recalled before the book was written. Since he's no longer around to straighten out my priorities, I'll have to return to these pages for Red's lessons.

Red wanted his life and his career on his own terms. He demanded it. He stood up for principles and he paid the price. He struggled to make people who weren't there understand the times. And even though he outlived most of the people who could contradict him on the facts, it's ultimately a losing battle; in the end, our stories are told by others.

This is not a biography. I have included some biographical information because many of our conversations dealt with his life and career. I have attempted to tell the only story I know—the story of the twelve years we had. Though he seemed to have an encyclopedic memory, the Red Barber I knew was an old man with zest for the present and hope for the future. His biographers will have to find that younger Red, the wiry little guy at the peak of his game, the fellow who gave stations, networks, sponsors, ad agencies and ball clubs all they could handle, the private man who lived a public life. I wish them luck.

Red Barber was a very complicated person who would not fit neatly into one of his simple sermons. There were layers and layers to the man. His daughter, Sarah, knows a Red I'll never know. Scully, Allen, Harwell and the others who worked with him know another Red. They all had perspectives different from mine, and probably no single perspective is entirely accurate.

Not everyone liked him. This may be hard for some of

his NPR listeners to believe, for they were so fond of the kindly old gent from Tallahassee. But Red was a first-class boat-rocker. He did not accept things that were handed to him if they could be improved. He could not work with people who didn't give their absolute best. His mother taught him to appreciate quality, so he could not tolerate mediocrity. Aiming for high standards is admirable, but it didn't endear him to the people he pushed to excellence. It also provided opportunities for his rivals to sling mud. Tom Gallery was director of sports at NBC when Red had the same job at CBS. In Curt Smith's book *Voices of the Game,* sportscaster Lindsey Nelson quotes Gallery as saying of Red, "I hate that Psalm-singing, sanctimonious son of a bitch." With such a gift for alliteration, Gallery should have been writing for Spiro Agnew.

One of the many contradictions about working in broadcast journalism is that we want to be liked, but we're working in jobs that tend to make us unpopular. Popularity brings ratings, which are important to longevity on the job, but journalism is about telling the truth, and some people don't always want to hear the truth. Others want the truth bent to suit their politics. One might be tempted to bend the truth and be popular, but to do so is to be worthless as a reporter. Red Barber did not compromise the truth. It was what it was and couldn't be helped. He retained his popularity with the public, though not always with those closest to him. Those of us committed to telling the truth are not always willing to hear it from our colleagues. I think Red believed that couldn't be helped.

Red's success began when he stopped trying to be someone else and focused on being himself. He was a Southerner, and Southerners are ridiculed and parodied even today. Imagine what it took for Red to cut through the early radio preference for voices free of any accent, color or regionalism. It wasn't any easier in the fifties and sixties when a Southern accent reminded people of the sheriffs and governors who were the heavies on the nightly news.

Yet there was Red, the Andy Griffith of sports broadcasting, based in the media capital of the nation, broadcasting
the games of the New York *Yankees*. A sitting duck in the
catbird seat! But he was a Southern man who demanded to
be accepted on his own terms.

The successful person is a prime target, and not just for
jealous rivals who want success for themselves. There always seem to be people anxious to take the hero down a
peg or two. Walter O'Malley and Mike Burke had brilliant
careers, yet they're smaller men to me for what they did to
Red. Craig Smith? Only his family will remember that Gillette executive for anything other than treating Red Barber as a peon. Burke didn't give Red a chance to grovel,
but what if Red had rolled over for the others? Would we
blame him? Red wouldn't have cared what we thought;
Red cared what *he* thought about himself.

He was a twentieth-century man, and was here for what
historians regard as the bookends for the period: World
War I and the demise of the Soviet Union. As Frank Deford said on *Morning Edition*, "It must not have been easy
to ride shotgun for the twentieth-century United States.
But the ones who managed it best instructed us a great
deal, and Walter Lanier Barber has certainly been one of
the most special of them." I thought a lot about that when
my father, Joe Edwards, died in March of 1991. His generation had two world wars sandwiching the Great Depression. They survived all the ugliness they were dealt and
delivered us into a rather prosperous time. I'm not sure we
ever thanked them. I do remember that we told them their
values were screwed up. Red could not help but be shaped
by his times and his heritage, but unlike some of his contemporaries, he could examine himself and see what
needed changing.

A twentieth-century discovery diverted him from be-
coming a teacher. And I cannot think of radio and Red
Barber without thinking of Red's first boss at CBS, Edward
R. Murrow, another Southern man whose rise and fall

paralleled Red's. Murrow called radio "that most satisfying and rewarding instrument." He preached that because we had been given this marvelous technology enabling us to speak to millions all over the world, we should not get the impression that it filled us with any more insight or wisdom than we had when our voices carried only as far as the other end of the bar. Red followed that philosophy, too. He admitted mistakes. Humility and self-effacing humor were part of his charm (though a few of his associates said that was only the Barber we heard on the air). Murrow and Barber helped invent reporting for television, and both knew instantly that they could never do the reporting job on TV that they could do on radio.

In eulogizing Murrow, Eric Sevareid said, "He was a shooting star and we shall not see his like again." He could say that in absolute confidence because Sevareid knew that the time, the place, the circumstances and the man could never repeat themselves in broadcast journalism. So it is with Red Barber and broadcast sports journalism. Murrow and Barber set the standards for their respective roles in the industry. The standards were tough ones and there are plenty of us who don't mind following those standards. These, too, are gifts left behind. But the people running the business today don't want to hear about them. Wall Street takeovers, competition from cable TV and the MTV generation's short attention span for public affairs have changed the rules. There is no room for a Murrow or a Barber in commercial broadcasting today.

The world moves on. Institutions change and entire industries die as new ones emerge. Red took pleasure in the things that endure, for quality is timeless. He found beauty in *Aida*, in a Julio Nudzio camellia, in fine literature, in the Old Testament and in a Reese-to-Robinson-to-Hodges double play. The moral lessons of man, the beauty of nature and the inspiration of art are the elements that make civilization better. They were there for us yesterday and they'll be there for us tomorrow.

Red Barber's ashes now are part of the Florida soil. His body couldn't last, but there's not another thing about him that has to die. He gave me lessons that are easy to relate here on these pages, and others I'll recall when I need them. I'll be quoting him as often as he told us about Branch Rickey and Larry MacPhail. He'll be with me the rest of my life.

On my desk is a picture of the smiling young Red Barber who worked at WRUF in Gainesville. Behind that photo is another one of an old Red Barber retired in Tallahassee. I think Red's ultimate lesson—perhaps the real gift—is that we can get from one photo to the other with a certain style and grace and humor.

Colonel Bob is not Red's broadcasting heir. But like everyone who ever heard him, I am his beneficiary.

Bibliography

Barber, Lylah, *Lylah,* Algonquin Books of Chapel Hill, Chapel Hill, North Carolina, 1985.

Barber, Red, *The Rhubarb Patch,* with pictures by Barney Stein, Simon and Schuster, New York, 1954.

Barber, Red, *Walk in the Spirit,* The Dial Press, New York, 1969.

Barber, Red, *The Broadcasters,* The Dial Press, New York, 1970.

Barber, Red, *Show Me the Way to Go Home,* The Westminster Press, Philadelphia, 1971.

Barber, Red, *1947—When All Hell Broke Loose in Baseball,* Doubleday & Company, Inc., Garden City, New York, 1982.

Barber, Red, and Robert Creamer, *Rhubarb in the Catbird Seat,* Doubleday & Company, Inc., Garden City, New York, 1968.

Caudill, Orley B., interview with Red Barber for the Mississippi Oral History Program of the University of Southern Mississippi, February 27, 1973.

Creamer, Robert, *Baseball in '41,* Viking, New York, 1991.

Deford, Frank, commentary on NPR's *Morning Edition,* October 1992.

Golenbock, Peter, *Bums,* G. P. Putnam's Sons, New York, 1984.

Harwell, Ernie, *Tuned to Baseball,* Diamond Communications, Inc., South Bend, Indiana, 1985.

Holmes, Tommy, *The Dodgers,* Collier Books, New York, 1975.

Kahn, Roger, *The Boys of Summer,* Harper & Row, New York, 1972.

Lelchuk, Alan, *Brooklyn Boy,* McGraw-Hill, New York, 1990.

Littlefield, Bill, commentary on WBUR-FM, Boston, October 1992.

Marshall, William J., "Baseball from the Catbird Seat: An Interview with Walter 'Red' Barber," *The Kentucky Review,* vol. 10, no. 2, Summer 1990.

Masterson, Dave, and Timm Boyle, *Baseball's Best: The MVP's,* Contemporary Books, Chicago, 1985.

Polner, Murray, *Branch Rickey,* Atheneum, New York, 1982.

Reichler, Joseph L., editor, *The Baseball Encyclopedia,* sixth edition, Macmillan Publishing Company, New York, 1985.

Smith, Curt, *Voices of the Game,* Diamond Communications, Inc., South Bend, Indiana, 1987.

Tygiel, Jules, *Baseball's Great Experiment: Jackie Robinson and His Legacy,* Oxford University Press, New York, 1983.

Index